WHAT DE FELLENBERG HAS DONE FOR EDUCATION.

LONDON:

SAUNDERS AND OTLEY, CONDUIT STREET.

1839.

LONDON:
PRINTED BY LEVEY, ROBSON, AND FRANKLYN,
46 St. Martin's Lane.

INTRODUCTORY REMARKS.

The name of De Fellenberg is familiar to all the civilised nations of Europe and North America, and may now be mentioned without offence. This expression implies that it once was otherwise. Yes; the age in which he has lived having been one of political storms, every name which was eminent enough to appear above the surface of the troubled waters was claimed or denounced by a party; none could escape. Even those who disclaimed all party, but who, from the highest motives, thought they were bound not to live for themselves alone, nor to hide their talent in a napkin, but to labour, like the holy men of old, according to the light given them, for the permanent good of their fellow-creatures, were exposed to a moral martyrdom, from the ignorance, misconception, and hostility of their contemporaries.

Schools and education had certainly been heard

of from the times of Rome and Greece—had not been totally destroyed at the fall of the Empire—and had in a degree revived with the revival of learning: but the kind of education which Fellenberg contemplated, with its application to the lowest as well as the highest class of society, was so new, that it is still a novelty in enlightened England, after his forty years' experimental labours at Hofwyl. The great object to which he had determined to devote his life was the practical solution of the question, whether it is possible to influence and form the human character by early discipline and instruction; to set the motives, feelings, and passions, in a proper course; to fix in the mind moral and religious principles, giving rise to corresponding habits of action; to store the mind with just ideas, and the heart with Christian sentiments. He wished to raise the school from a mere technical system to one of intelligence; and from a place of irksome constraint to one of pleasing and beneficial occupations.

As these objects had never been attained, nor even attempted, with a direct, specific, and undivided purpose, Fellenberg's wise and benevolent plans for the improvement of character were looked at as dangerous innovations in the usual mode of bringing up the young, and as connected with some deep, secret plot for the subversion of society. He had, therefore, to contend, during many years, with a combination of ignorance, prejudice, and, we fear we must add, in some instances, of malignity. Before his time, almost the only medium of instruction for the people was the pulpit; almost the only means of discipline, of training and forming character, were domestic; which domestic training consisted in a short intercourse between parent and child at certain hours of the day, when labour was over; and in permitting the children, during the rest of the day, to wander at large in the streets of towns, or the fields of the country, encouraging each other to vice and impiety. It was this pernicious training which Fellenberg proposed to supersede by one of order, method, and discipline; to put useful employment in the place of mischievous idleness, and hourly Christian instruction and superintendence in the place of total neglect and ignorance. Was such a scheme feasible? and if so, would it not be better and more Christian than the former state of things?

Fellenberg was led to study this question in consequence of observing the state of Europe, at that time convulsed by the French revolution. The ambition of political power was the moving principle of the few, to which the many were made subservient; and the lives of all, instead of being passed in the exercise of peaceful virtues, with the hope and expectation of a better world, were exhausted in the rage and passions of savages. Fellenberg groaned over this exhibition of human ferocity,—over the social ruin which it occasioned,—over the total absence of Christian character which it betrayed. He beheld Christian men, as they called themselves, tearing one another to pieces, and for no ostensible good,— the mere instruments of the few ringleaders of the world's misery. Human nature seemed to have discarded all virtue, and to have become the receptacle of that assemblage of vices denounced by the apostle —" envy, variance, wrath, strife, hatred, sedition, drunkenness, revellings, adultery, murder."

Fellenberg at first imagined that something might be done among the rulers of mankind, the directors of the political storm, to calm this turbulent state, and to introduce harmony into this chaos; but he found them totally indifferent and apathetic, and blind to all but the scene in which they lived. Every man forms a horizon for himself by his actions, thoughts, and reading. The demagogue sees nothing but the mob before him; the soldier, nothing but the battle; the politician, often, especially in troublous times, nothing but the intrigues around him. None but the Christian philanthropist can take an enlarged view of man in his present and future hopes — his social condition, his capabilities of improvement, the possible extent of happiness or misery for which he may be born. The Bible presents him with the ideal perfectibility of universal man; inspiring those who drink deep into its spirit with high and noble hopes for the welfare of humanity, and with an ardent desire to promote it; while those who are wholly absorbed in the business of life remain pagans in a Christian age, and all their ideas of man are mean, low, and perishing: to them man still continues " a brute that perishes." Fellenberg, therefore, found no sympathy from the statesmen of his day; they were callous to the common social rights of states and of men, as well as indifferent to all views and projects of moral improvement. In fact, what does the mere politician, whether demagogue or tyrant, require of man, but to be a blind instrument in his ambitious grasp? He wishes his follower to have enough mind to direct his physical strength most effectually according to the command of a superior, but no more. It is the enlightened politician—the legislator properly so called—who considers man not as a tool with which he is to work, but as a ward committed to his charge, and for whose character, usefulness, and happiness, he will be held responsible at the day of judgment.

Fellenberg living in such an age of vice, impiety, and misery, felt keenly the degradation and corruption of man; and also that this was no new state of things, though an aggravated one. He saw that Europe had never been practically Christianised; that she had been converted from paganism little more than in name; and that her barbarism had never been extirpated. He beheld in history a swarm of nations issuing from savage forests, conquering a comparatively civilised nation, separating into feudalities, continuing their wars with each other, ignorant of letters, studying no art or science but that of the sword. The outbreakings of modern revolutions were nothing but a continuance of the history of the race. It was no new or sudden volcano, acting by new and unknown laws: the causes were deeply laid in the ignorance and barbarism of the people, and in the pugnacious and arbitrary principles of the rulers. We are not here questioning the providential wisdom of the history of man, as shewn in the European march from barbarism and paganism to civilisation, Christianity, and rational and constitutional liberty: but we cannot insist too strongly upon our pristine barbarism and ignorance, and the total want of any general moral means of removing them, beyond the formalities of religion; lest it should be imagined that the mass of the people among our ancestors were in possession of ample and efficient means of moral and religious instruction.

Fellenberg was one of the few who traced the tumults and troubles of his age to the moral depravity of men in their social relations. With the Bible in his hand, and an enlightened philosophy in his heart, he considered society and men as they were in fact, as they ought to be as Christians, and as they might be under a proper guidance and system of early discipline and instruction. Unlike others who had preceded him, but with partial and theoretic views of the subject, he did not propound his ideas to the public in writing; but, convinced of the truth, power, and force of the principles he had arrived at, he determined upon submitting them to the test of an experiment, to which he pledged his talents, property, and life,—and for so doing was denounced as the enemy of his race!

The improvement of mankind in the arts of civilisation seems to be under laws of more certain, or, rather, more rapid operation, than their improvement in morals. The civilisation of arts seems to be first attained; that of intellect next; and that of morals last of all. Indeed, the two former may advance while the latter seems to retrograde. This was the case among the early Eastern nations, and among the Greeks and Romans: so much so, that it became a kind of philosophical proverb, that when nations had attained to what was then deemed their highest point of so-called civilisation and refinement, they retrograded and declined by a natural necessity. The most civilised nations of Europe seem to have attained, during the last century, about the same degree of refinement which belonged to Greece and Rome in their best days. They were great in arms, arts, oratory, and poetry; but they had not improved in morals in an equal degree. They had, indeed, theoretically a better religion; but the superstitions of barbarous times were not worn out, the reformation of a corrupt creed was only partially effected;

and the peculiar sublimity of the Christian code of morals, the conquest over the selfish principle of man, and the exaltation of his motives into a dependence upon Divine direction and assistance, opening to him a field of progressive and infinite improvement, were almost unknown. Vice abounded in all classes of society, according to the circumstances, opportunities, and temptations of each; and the few holy characters which were scattered through the mass, seemed to be entirely isolated, and to exert no leavening process upon the surrounding crowds. At one time, vice was the test of loyalty, as piety was of disaffection; and the spread of infidelity was by some considered as a sign of national prosperity. We venture to say, that these feelings and judgments are not yet extinct. In our own age, it has been scarcely creditable to belong to Bible or missionary societies; and infant-schools were once considered as the nurseries of freethinkers, or as the visionary projects of Utopian philanthropists. It seemed to be absolutely necessary that mankind should experience practically the utmost horrors, misery, and anarchy of vice and ignorance, and have that experience reiterated upon them generation after generation, before they could be convinced of the inherent and indefeasible malignity of vice, and of the sublime beauty of holiness. The French revolution did indeed strike terror into the hearts of men, and made crime at length detestable. Not that it was the first or only consequence of vicious principles which Europe had witnessed—far from it—for she was bred in war and rapine; but vice appeared in a new garb, and less under the direction of its usual leaders. Still, the horror that was felt was more political than moral. Men feared the miseries of vice as exhibited in public convulsions; but they continued blind to its effects on social and domestic happiness. Provided the state were free from change, they cared not for the tears shed in secret over the degradation of private infamy. Another step was necessary in the moral demonstration; which was, that public prosperity and security should be deemed to be utterly incompatible with private vice.

To arrive practically at this momentous conclusion is a great era in the history of man, because it leads at once to a practical inquiry of an experimental kind; and when men are once bent upon an experimental pursuit, universal experience proves that their labours will be rewarded with a rich harvest.

Slow are men to be convinced of the importance and necessity of moral character to the security and prosperity of states; but slower still are they to discover in what way that moral character can be attained. The subject of the formation of character among the mass of mankind is altogether new. The characters of men have been formed in past times by national circumstances, and not at all by artificial means. By artificial means, we understand schools. There are only two means of forming character—the domestic hearth and the school. The former is evidently suited only to nations in a barbarous or semi-barbarous state. When men have advanced to a certain point of civilisation, the parents among the mass of the people are too much occupied in their daily callings to be able to influence their children sufficiently. The children then cease to imbibe the instructions or character of the parent, and come under the irregular and mischievous influence of each other; the parents also themselves, in passing from the barbarous to the civilised state, contract the vices peculiar to the latter. Every state of society is harassed by its peculiar vices, of which the mass are the victims. The domestic teaching, therefore, soon becomes worse than nothing—it is only a name. Under that name, the children of neighbouring families herd together, and contaminate each other. The character of man is habit: what, then, more fatal than the association of human beings, without the practice of virtue and prudence; without self-denial and experience; full of passion and irregular desire; and without control and discipline? Profligacy and recklessness must be the inevitable consequences. If there were not some unknown check upon this state of society, some providential superintendence, permitting all evils to have a certain sway and no more, with a view to the ultimate extermination of evil through its own odiousness, we should be filled with despair at the moral prospects of man under such circumstances, and foresee nothing but increasing vice and increasing political convulsion.

We have said, that parents, as soon as society passes from the barbarous state to the pursuit of arts, are totally incompetent to educate their own children, and that the artificial education of the school must commence. This is true of all classes of society, as well as of the lowest. Education becomes an art, as well as the manufacture of articles of consumption. It becomes subject to the law of the division of labour; and they who engage in it will excel in it by the same necessity that a mechanic excels in his peculiar occupation. Upon this principle, schools become necessary for all classes, to supply the want of time, attention, and knowledge, in parents of all ranks. If mankind had been capable of anticipating and foreseeing their own wants before they were pressed upon them by a painful experience, schools and schoolmasters would have been coeval with the first transition from a state of barbarian war to one of incipient civilisation and the cultivation of the arts. But man cannot foresee, and can only learn by pain and sorrow how to obviate the recurrence of similar suffering. The formation of character by means of schools,—*i.e.* by means of systematic discipline and instruction,—is a new thought. Schools were first established for other purposes; and when established, the formation of character was not an element in their system, nor is it so yet. Schools were established for the sake of mere knowledge; for cultivating the intellect, not the heart. The progress of society required a certain number of persons who could read and write, in order to fill, in church and state, certain offices which had sprung up from the necessities of society;

and it was long before these necessities were really supplied. Of those who were thus educated, some turned their attention to literature and general knowledge, and thus opened a new field for the employment of the human mind—a field of mere abstract knowledge and speculation, totally unconnected with practical purposes.

But by the same condition that the practical position of government and of the church required that a certain number of persons should receive what was called a learned education, the position of affairs in the middle classes of society also began to make some education appear desirable. Persons were not fitted to carry on the common business of life without a certain amount of instruction; and as only one kind was to be had, men were obliged to send their children to the schools which happened to be in existence. These schools were all of the same character: the subjects taught, and the mode of teaching, were the same, whatever condition of life the pupils were intended for; and this system was a necessary one under the circumstances, because some of the scholars being intended for the learned professions, as they were called, became the principal objects of the master's care. He adapted his system to them; and the others were obliged to follow it, and to make the best of it, though it might not be the best preparation for them and their professions, as it was supposed to be for others.

In order to understand the history of schools, and to make allowance for the defects of the early ones, and through this history to improve our own, we must consider that the early schools were confined in the materials they had to work with. These were few and scanty both in kind and degree. Every science and art had to be discovered before it could be taught: grammar and logic, geography and maps, arithmetic, geometry, and natural philosophy, elementary history, the mythology of the classics, illustrations of manners and customs, dictionaries,—every thing had to be constructed; so that it is wonderful what and how the early schools contrived to teach. The subjects taught, and the mode of teaching, had to undergo a progress of discovery and improvement, like all other sciences. It might have been expected, the teachers should have discovered what they were most in want of; but we should bear in mind, that their time and thoughts are occupied not in discovering, but in teaching. Many of the most important materials of teaching are derived from other professions. The teacher only selects and concentrates what he finds useful to his purpose. The early schools, of necessity exceedingly imperfect, have unfortunately entailed their imperfections upon their successors. The objects they contemplated were unfavourable to enlarged views, or to any thing like an educational system. With them education was a mere apprenticeship to the learned languages—a mere trade, not a science. They professed to teach one thing, and one thing only, the grammatical elements of Latin, and, perhaps, of Greek. We say elements, because that degree of teaching which consists in writing and speaking those languages with facility, has hardly yet been attained in any school. This leads us to consider a wonderful fact, that, though every child learns to talk his own language while he is a child, yet, after ten years' teaching of the Latin or Greek language, the scholar has not learnt to speak, and scarcely to write it. The withering effects of this contracted system of teaching, this limiting of instruction to Greek and Latin, were not so much felt in the higher departments of society, for which it was chiefly intended, because such instruction occupied only a portion of a long period of pupilage, and because no other knowledge or science was required in some of the professions; while in others, personal labour and perseverance made up for all deficiencies of elementary teaching. And we must never forget that the innate powers, faculties, and principles of the human mind, are not to be judged of by the results of any teaching which has hitherto prevailed. Teaching cannot create: mind is a creation. Teaching is only moulding that which already exists; and this moulding, if not conducted skilfully, and agreeably with the original laws and intentions of the Creator, will only deface his work, instead of bringing it to its intended perfection. The mind of original ability and talent, therefore, made its way amid all difficulties, and amid the vices of all teaching, to its proper station in the world of mind, and was no proof of any excellence in the system under which it was trained. With the majority of minds it was far different. A contracted and dry system was to them a second nature, and frustrated the first which they had received at birth; and the faults of the teaching were imputed to the original creation. Thus nature became libelled by the very persons who ought to have worshipped her: the beauties they had defaced were pronounced never to have existed, and the distortions of art were asserted to be natural deformities.

The incurable and ruinous consequences of this contracted system were seen and first remedied in the profession of arms. As the art of war became a science, and dependent upon mind more than upon brute force, real knowledge, a knowledge of arithmetic and geometry, became the only basis upon which it could be erected. Government was therefore obliged to establish schools of its own, adapted to its purpose; not merely schools for completing education, analogous to universities, but elementary schools for teaching the simplest properties of numbers and space. When other persons demanded that these elements should be made a part of teaching in schools, they were pronounced unnecessary and useless, except for certain mechanic arts. When admitted, they were taught by permission rather than upon principle, and a certain air of contempt was thrown over them. Elements upon which depended the perfection of the art of war and national security and independence, and upon which the whole fabric of the universe was created, were pronounced to be contemptible, and are still held in all the higher English schools to be of very inferior importance.

The middling classes of society also at length perceived the imperfect and inadequate teaching of the schools. At the age when parents were obliged to remove their children from school, they found them not only deficient in all knowledge calculated to prove practically useful in the employments for which they were destined, but even in that to which their time had been solely devoted. Not to have been taught useful practical knowledge, was an evil; but, not to have been taught that which alone had been attempted, was more serious still. These middling classes, however, had not the power, like government, of correcting these evils: they could not establish schools and professorships of their own; neither their time nor their funds allowed of it. They were compelled to accept what the schools offered, and to make the best of it. Fortunately the consequences, however injurious, were not so fatal as they would have proved in the other case, had that also been without a remedy. Inferior and limited teaching rendered them a less intelligent class of people, less skilful in their employments, less capable of improving their situation and circumstances, less useful members of the community, with fewer resources, fewer means of self-recreation and rational amusement, and left their moral character much lower than it ought to have been; but it did not expose these classes to absolute ruin, as would have been the case with the nation, had government not taken the education of its military servants out of the hands of the common schools.

We have called the schools of former days a system of mere teaching, because of their confined plan, objects, and attainments; we have now to consider what they were as places of education. School and education are thought to be synonymous terms; and so they ought to be—but so it has not been. Education is a term of wide signification, and will not apply, except in a most qualified manner, to any narrow or partial system. A system which merely proposes to teach one particular art, science, or language, is not an education, except in a very loose acceptation. All the early period of life, up to the time when a person enters upon a profession or a business, is the period of education. In whatever way he may be taught or managed during that period, that teaching and management is called his education, however imperfect or even objectionable it may be. In one sense, every thing which happens to a person, from the cradle to the period of his entering on active and responsible life, may be very justly called his education; because, by all those circumstances, whatever they may be, whether good or bad, favourable or unfavourable, in a school or out of a school, private or public, his habits and character are formed, and he becomes a good or bad member of society. But true education contemplates the whole man,—not one faculty alone, but all his faculties, powers, feelings, and principles; so that the word is of wide import, and may include either the very highest or the very lowest set of circumstances in which a human being may be brought up. It is necessary to bear in mind this expansive meaning of the term, because it affects every argument on the subject, and entirely alters its complexion, according as it is applied to the higher or lower classes of the community. Thus a person who has low and contracted ideas of education will call any school-instruction an education, however few may be the subjects taught, or however imperfect the method of teaching. In speaking of even the highest schools, he will consider their education perfect, because they stand high in public estimation, without inquiring into the details of the system followed, or its effect upon the character and principles. Some people have no idea of any education beyond the bare teaching of the classics, and will hence condemn the education of the lower classes; as if there was nothing else which they might profitably learn, and as if education had nothing to do with the formation of character independently of learning Latin and Greek.

To have a worthy conception of all that is meant by the term *education*, we must not be content with a dictionary, and call it with Johnson, " the instruction of children;" but we must consider what man is in his original and divine faculties, what is the calling for which he is destined in this life, and what are the ultimate expectations and responsibilities of his being in the life to come. Education brings out all the faculties of man with a view to the two great ends of his being, both present and future; to his own personal happiness, and to the good of society. If there is one feature in education more prominent than another, it is this, that it involves moral and religious character more than intellect. It is the connexion of education with character, and the great dependence of the one upon the other, which renders the subject of universal interest and of unbounded importance.

This view of education has only of late began to be generally taken. The early schools were entirely intellectual. They proposed to themselves only the cultivation of the intellectual powers, talents, and abilities, in a restricted sense; and they only attempted to educate for the demands of the day, which were some knowledge of the Latin and Greek languages. There was a historical reason for this: the records of revelation were enclosed in these languages; those records could only be understood and fairly estimated by the study of their languages. They had been the mother-tongue of the first disciples of the religion, and of the great works of the first scholars, and orators, and, we might almost say, philosophers, which had adorned it. They contained what may be called its early literature and external history. When, therefore, our Germanic forefathers were sufficiently civilised to begin the acquisition of literature, they were compelled, by the moral necessity of circumstances, to cultivate the Latin and Greek languages; and schools were compelled, in like manner, to make those languages their principal, if not their only subject of instruction. Thus education became identified with the study of those two languages, and the name and thing were defined in accordance with this narrow, but, at that period, not unimportant purpose. To teach *them*, was to educate; and to be educated, was to have been at a school where they were taught. After the demand for persons so educated had been supplied, and persons intended for other professions, and for the middle walks of life, began to frequent these schools—and after some other kinds of knowledge began to creep into them,—as such knowledge grew up in the world, and came also into demand, the same intellectual character continued to possess the schools. The training of the moral habits was not considered to be the chief, or even a leading end to be aimed at.

The same necessity which compelled persons who were intended for the higher professions to study Latin and Greek, compelled other classes to make different acquisitions of knowledge. Thus reading, writing, and the first elements of numbers, became absolutely necessary for a certain number of people of all classes, as the affairs of common life became more complicated, and as trade and commerce extended. Schools, therefore, for teaching these elements alone, descended to the lowest ranks, from which indeed—such was the demand for this knowledge—many persons arose, who, by ability, industry, and perseverance, attained to wealth and celebrity, and laid the foundation of influential families in the kingdom. But the numbers of such schools were still small compared with the whole population, and worldly utility was the chief end proposed in them both by master and scholar. How it happened that so much time was consumed in making such trifling attainments, may now appear extraordinary; but the art of teaching was in its infancy, and consisted chiefly in giving children an opportunity of teaching themselves, rather than in directing or contributing to their acquirements. The greater part of the school-time was occupied in doing nothing. Children were confined within doors during certain hours, whether occupied or not; and with this so-called teaching all parties were satisfied, if we except the scholars, who, employed upon dull, irksome, and often unintelligible tasks, never tasted the sweets of knowledge, of which none was imparted—did not feel, that, even in their avowed studies, they made any progress, and therefore considered school only as a species of imprisonment.

The last half century has seen such changes in European society, manners, habits, education, arts, and sciences, as cannot be paralleled in the history of mankind. One of its grandest features has been a moral one: it has been the era of Bibles. In all ages of the Christian dispensation, missionaries have been sent forth, more or less, to announce the glad tidings of salvation to all lands; but in none has the Bible itself been sent forth to be its own herald, with or without the accompanying missionary, with the same zeal or to the same extent. In no former age had it been felt, that nations of professing Christians might be enveloped in pagan darkness as much as those who never heard the name of Christ; and that the possession, and therefore the spirit of the Bible, was in many Christian places as rare as in pagan land. This was a great *moral discovery*, however strong the term may appear to be; and the men who could make and feel the value of that discovery possessed no ordinary mind and heart, and were an earnest of the moral spirit which was awakening from its slumbers. This spirit could not fail to diffuse itself into all those subjects which concern the character, happiness, and improvement of man. It should have been watched, appreciated, and directed, instead of being confounded with a mere revolutionary mania. If, indeed, this spirit had not sprung up, all Europe would probably have run the same course of " decline and fall" as did the empires of old. The Bible stood between us and the precipice, and saved the world politically, as the divine Author of Christianity had saved it morally.

It was this moral spirit which prompted the education of the people at large—of the lowest order of society, as they have been called. Education had begun to spread among this class beyond the mere demand for it of which we have spoken; but it was expensive, and extremely imperfect, even in imparting the trifling elements of reading, writing, and arithmetic. The importance, however, of this degree of education, as the handmaid of religion and morality, was beginning to be perceived; and though the ostensible object was principally the acquisition of the elements of knowledge, the real object was an ulterior one—namely, the improvement of character, and the acquisition of Christian instruction. When it was discovered that, by proper arrangements, one master might teach the elements to three hundred, or even five hundred children, as perfectly as to a few, the moral spirit of the day was roused to carry such a system into practice; and the magnificent idea occurred of giving to every Christian child a Christian education.

The era of popular education had therefore begun—it was the companion of the Bible era. Both had the same object in view; the moral improvement of all mankind, of the universal race, as far as might be permitted by the conditions of this imperfect stage of existence. The one was the foundation, the other the superstructure; the one was the light of the world, the other the guide by which that light was, humanly speaking, to be reached and disseminated.

But the schools established upon this principle could imitate at first none but those which preceded them in their immediate object, which was, as we have said, more intellectual than moral. They proposed to improve the methods of attaining the elements of knowledge; and though the Bible was introduced as a class-book, yet the mode in which it was read partook more of an intellectual than of a moral exercise. Spelling-lessons were made from it, and detached parts were extracted for reading-lessons, which lost much of their force by being separated from the context; and sometimes sentences were associated for the mere purpose of learning to read, having no connexion in sense with each other. Besides, it is very possible to learn to spell and read, without having any comprehension of the sense. At this day, the children of those who speak the Gaelic language in Scotland are taught to read English fluently, without understanding it. The effects of these schools, therefore, were less perfect than had been anticipated, though as good as, under all the circumstances, could be expected by those who had a practical knowledge of early education, and of the intricacies of the human mind, and of the numerous difficulties to be overcome, before the results of education can be reduced to any thing like certainty. An opinion is now very generally gaining ground, that these schools have not attained all that was desirable, and that their methods require and are susceptible of improvement—that they have been too exclusively intellectual and mechanical—that they do not sufficiently influence the moral habits, and therefore the religious principles of the children. The term *education* is beginning to be understood in its full and legitimate sense, as affecting the whole character of the man, moral as well as intellectual, but principally the former; that its great end and aim should be to form good practical principles and habits, and not great readers or arithmeticians: and these ideas have spread from the lower to the higher schools. Men may be useful and happy with inferior literary attainments, but not with inferior moral principles and habits. The miseries of the world in past ages have been occasioned by its vices, not by its ignorance of languages, arts, and sciences, any farther than as the latter may influence the former. There is a growing conviction that the great antidote to vice and crime, and therefore to political disturbances, is to be found in an improved moral education in the mass of the people.

We have thus traced the history of education in Europe, according to our own impressions of it, because the principles of such subjects are only to be found in their history. Imagination is fond of looking forward to the future in its own poetic dreams, without studying the past; but the true future can only be seen in the past, of which it is the necessary consequence. The facts of past ages contain the moral laws of man, as determined by his Creator; and the sagacious development of those laws indicates the finger of Providence. The history of schools must not be looked at merely in themselves, but as proofs of the character of the successive ages; and by studying the demands of this character in past ages, we may foretell, to a certain extent, its future demands. Schools, as well as all other institutions, are formed by the general character of the times, which is in a great measure independent of all things but itself. While it acts on all things, it is no doubt reacted upon by them, in a degree; but it is itself the great mainspring, the great source of vitality. Man was made to govern the world and to serve his Maker; and for both purposes he must have an original independent character stamped upon him, the law of which is self-expansive, both in the individual and in the mass, advancing from generation to generation, " conquering and to conquer." We have demonstrable proof of this both in philosophy and in revelation; for revelation was evidently intended to bring man from a state of pagan barbarism into one of civilisation and social blessings—to carry him beyond what any mere social institutions could do—to give him new springs of action from within himself—to raise him to a sense of his individual importance in the sight of his Maker—to give him a more penetrating moral eye, and a wider moral horizon—to elevate him from matter to spirit, from sense to mind, from the impure and the grovelling to the pure, the holy, and the sublime,—and to make the mortal and finite forgotten in the immortal and the infinite.

Let us now apply the preceding considerations to the character of Fellenberg. It is about thirty years since the idea of popular education took root in this country; and it is only as yesterday that the full meaning of the term *education*, as implying the formation of principles and character, began to be understood; but it is forty years since the subject was viewed by Fellenberg in all its bearings and importance. To arrive at his conclusions, to satisfy himself of the improvableness of man, and of the methods by which such possible improvement was to be attained, required great honesty of mind, strong religious principles, a genuine philanthropy and gospel-love of his fellow-creatures, great knowledge of the principles of human nature, a thorough sense and conviction of the deplorable moral state of man, a deep philosophical spirit, and a perfect disinterestedness. It was necessary that he should look into himself for all the resources of which he had need. He could obtain help from no one: he could even obtain sympathy from no one. His views, when proposed to others, would appear fanciful, Utopian, and impracticable. If they had been simple and obvious, he would not have been the first to entertain them. For the very reason that he was the first to conceive the practical improvement of mankind, he was not understood; not being understood, he was misrepresented and attacked. This is no new circumstance in the history of man; ignorance, misconception, misrepresentation, opposition, hatred, persecution, follow each other in a necessary order. The passions of men follow their motives, their motives follow their knowledge. Ignorance therefore necessarily produces bad motives, and bad motives rouse bad passions. The enumeration and classification of motives, and the inculcation of good ones as the basis of character, had not yet entered into the conception of educators, except of Fellenberg. But Fellenberg was not to be daunted or deterred by any obstacles, physical or moral. He trusted in the soundness of his principles, in the holiness of his cause, and in the order of Providence. His feelings, motives, and principles, were fundamentally and essentially religious, though in working them out he appeared to be following a philosophical scheme, and to depend upon philosophical means and principles. This general mistake respecting his views and motives arose from the extremely imperfect education hitherto in operation, and the extremely imperfect method of instruction on all subjects—but especially on moral and religious ones—hitherto pursued at all schools. Words are considered merely grammatically as words, and not intellectually and morally as the representatives of thoughts, feelings, things, and events; and when the meaning of words is required or given, it is from the dictionary, a dry formal one—a distinction from other words rather than the development of the meaning and bearing of the word itself as the representative of things. Hence the extent to which men have been deceived and misled by the use and abuse of words. Partial and party meanings have been attached to them; and what were invented and intended originally to promote the knowledge of things, have often proved to be among the greatest obstacles to knowledge. The business of the savage is to invent words to express his thoughts, and feelings, and the objects he is acquainted with; that of the civilised man, of the scholar and man of intellect, is to form clear ideas of the things which are represented by all the words of the language he studies. The child is surrounded by and overwhelmed with words. He reads, especially in this age of books, words innumerable, whose sounds and letters he knows, but not their meanings. When questioned upon that subject, he shews the few ideas which the words have conveyed.

Those who first visited the establishment of Fellenberg saw a great scheme in action of schools, workshops, and agriculture; they saw new things taught, and old things taught in a new way; they saw schools for all classes, the lowest and the highest, carried on under one superintendence. When the establishment was explained to them, they heard the reasons of what was done, and the dependence of one part upon another. This was the explanation they desired, and the one which was obviously desirable to be given and received. They did not require, nor was it possible, that Fellenberg should enter into the history of his own mind upon the subject, and how far his religious and conscientious feelings had operated in urging him to the undertaking. They therefore denominated the whole machinery a piece of philosophy; and this ominous word was echoed through Europe — particularly through England — accompanied by all the vague, indefinite, and erroneous ideas which modern times had attached to it. Philosophy, which originally meant the study of wisdom, means specifically, in these days, the attempt to discover some rule or law under which a number of facts may be ranged, or to deduce some maxim of common sense from the study of a particular subject, by which our actions may be directed and regulated. The English pride themselves upon their practical common sense on all subjects, and upon their disregard of theory and philosophy, as unsuited to practice; but they forget that this is only philosophy under a different name, and that the greatest philosopher is he who can best adapt general rules and maxims to the practice of common life. If we glance at the state of crime— at that of pauperism a few years ago — and at the general results of education among the middle and upper classes,—we shall have no great reason to boast of our common sense, or of our wisdom in discarding the study of philosophy as applicable to the improvement of man.

It is a great thing to introduce the love of any subject or science into the heart; or to excite, in one's self or others, the sentiment of love at all. He who has it not, has only half a title to humanity; he who has once attained it, has entered into the highest class among the beings to which he belongs. For this truth we have the surest possible authority — that of the Divine Founder of our religion; love being made by him the grand test of discipleship. This love must be as diffusive as the works of its primary and great object, the Maker of all things. The sentiment which has once attached itself to him must spread over all his works; because wherever they are, He is, for they exist only in him. It even attaches itself to inanimate and insensible things; it sees "sermons in stones, and good in every thing." Much more does it unfold itself towards its own kind — towards the image of the Divinity, which is stamped upon every human being. A man may become an earnest politician, or a violent party-man, or a philosophical writer upon plausible theories of imaginary virtue, without any practical sentiment of regard and love for man, or of reverence for his Maker; but no man without that sentiment will engage in a scheme of benevolence entirely practical, which will require years of labour, anxiety, self-sacrifice, and expense, to bring to perfection. It is a common proverb, that it is easy to talk, but difficult to practise. If Fellenberg had been like other men, he would have been satisfied with writing or declaiming on these subjects; but he would not have retired from public life, that he might surround himself with objects of care and responsibility, and have drawn upon himself the suspicion and ill-will of his countrymen and of prejudiced foreigners.

We must not, however, omit to mention, that Fellenberg was preceded in his philanthropic path by one celebrated individual, Pestalozzi;* whose sensitive nature, shocked at the vice and brutality of the lowest class of society about him—filled with pity for the deserted and destitute state of the children—and deeply penetrated with the utter inefficiency of all the common methods of training them up to Christian virtue,—determined to try what methods entirely new might accomplish in saving them from destruction, vice, and infamy, and forming them to industry and religion. He simply assumed these principles—that children are created with minds, feelings, affections, a moral instinct, and an under-

* It should not be forgotten that Pestalozzi himself had been preceded by Rochow, Basedow, Campe, and Saltzmann; to each of whom education owes some improvement.

standing; that mere memory is one of the lowest of the faculties; that learning by rote, without the participation of the understanding, is not only useless and disgusting, but positively injurious, since it tends to weaken, and may even pervert, the judgment; that the exercise of the affections and understanding in a natural way must be agreeable and interesting to children; and that both nature and revelation must be delightful to the human soul, if presented to it in a proper manner. The problem to be solved was, How is this method to be discovered? Pestalozzi discarded at once the usual primary step of the alphabet and of spelling, and deferred them till a certain portion of knowledge had been acquired by oral instruction. Instead of letters, he presented to the children things themselves, and explained to them their nature and uses; their qualities, as perceived by the different senses; their uses in the common concerns of life; their natural history; how they were produced in nature; and what changes they underwent before they became applicable to different uses. In all this, the understanding preceded the memory; and the children were found to be born with a relish for knowledge which had never been suspected, and with an innate ability for acquiring it which had been thought to be the result only of a long and refined education. In like manner, instead of giving them moral precepts to commit to memory, he drew out their moral feelings by suitable questions, and by supposed cases of life and manners; by bringing before their imagination scenes of domestic life, family affection, good and bad conduct; and by applying the ideas, feelings, and principles, thus drawn forth, to their own behaviour one among another. When he had in this manner informed and enlightened the conscience and moral judgment, he brought his instruction to the test of Scripture, which he illustrated and enforced, and then impressed upon them as the highest moral authority, and one to which their whole nature should be subject. He next opened to them, after having thus prepared the way, the spirituality of their own nature, and the eternal improvement for which it had been created. He then returned to the first and simple principles from which he set out, and shewed how the exercise of the senses, and the knowledge obtained by them, were the first links in the chain of divine benevolence and wisdom, by which the young were both to lay hold of wisdom and happiness themselves, and to glorify Him who made and upheld them.

Pestalozzi could not fully explain his views of education or of human nature: he was surrounded with difficulties; those views were extensive, embracing man in all his faculties, feelings, and affections; in all his stages of childhood, youth, and maturity; in all his relations of child and parent, servant or master, subject or ruler; and as a religious being, looking forward to a responsible eternity. No man can appreciate education who does not view it in its whole extent. It is the contracted view of it, of which we have spoken before, that causes it to be misunderstood and undervalued. But to carry his plans into effect, Pestalozzi required time—the same individuals to be under his management during the whole period of education, till they should be old enough to enter upon active life: he required the means of maintaining his establishment, and teachers to assist imbued with his own views, and practically capable of acting upon them. Then he had to contend against the prejudices and self-interest of people about him — of the parents — of the Church to which he belonged — and of the public functionaries of the state—who were all jealous of new ideas, whatever they might be, and who feared that, however corrupted and vicious the people were, every attempt to improve them would only make them worse. Pestalozzi had neither the funds to support his establishment, nor health, strength, and calmness, to contend against the opposition he met with from those who misapprehended his views, or envied him the chance of success, or opposed him for mere party purposes. Thus, this great friend of humanity and practical religion became a martyr to the grand cause for which man was created and redeemed—the cause of moral regeneration and of the practical influence of the Gospel.

But Pestalozzi had not lived in vain. Though some of his pupils had repaid his kindness and confidence with base ingratitude, others had caught a ray of his spirit, and contributed to spread its light through Europe by various publications. No real friend of man should ever be disheartened at the slowness with which his good suggestions are understood and received by the world, nor at the obloquy through which they have to pass on their road to adoption. If a man can sow but " one grain of mustard-seed" during this his mortal pilgrimage, he may lay his head in peace upon the pillow of death, satisfied that he has not lived in vain. We cannot but believe that there is an especial providence over the hearts and lives of the moral improvers of mankind. " Every good gift and every perfect gift is from above, and cometh down from the Father of lights." Society could not hold on its progressive course without continual accessions of light and knowledge, exhibited and conveyed through the agencies of the zealous and disinterested lovers of their kind. These necessary and invaluable gifts are all rays from Divine wisdom. It is our business to study and profit by them, and to observe in them the general rule or law with which they are connected, in order to work with them for the improvement of man.

When Fellenberg, therefore, began to direct his mind to the formation of moral and religious character in youth, as the preventive remedy for vice and crime, and as the necessary steps, humanly speaking, of elevating the heart to Christian principles, he had the advantage of the experience of Pestalozzi, and of other less eminent men, which materially smoothed down the first difficulties of his path. It had been proved that children might be taken from the most abandoned parents, and after being for a certain time brought under the steady, judicious, and kind discipline of Pestalozzi, would become tractable, orderly, and industrious. Vice seemed to disappear spontaneously, and good conduct to take its place. Idleness ceased to possess charms; regular labour and mental cultivation became happiness. A spirit of Christian affection and Christian duty grew up among the pupils, and religious principles became motives of conduct.

Before Fellenberg began to act upon his views, he had arrived at the conclusion, that the only solid basis of human character was religion; but as man is compelled to work by means (and, indeed, means form also the mode of development of the Divine wisdom and power), he had to look to means for the attainment of his object—to contrive the various employments and mental tasks, and the whole system of management, which must pervade his establishment. Superficial observers imagined, when they beheld all this apparatus, that what was obvious to the senses constituted the whole of Fellenberg's ideas: because they did not see the soul of the machine, they concluded there was none; and because Fellenberg was not constantly sermonising his pupils —though religion was on all suitable occasions directly inculcated—they doubted his religious motives. No conclusion could be more illogical. Fellenberg ought to be allowed the same privilege which is enjoyed by all superintendents of a large and complicated plan. While examining it in detail, we are apt to forget one point in considering another; we are apt to overrate the relative importance of parts while inspecting them; we may differ in our opinion of the subordinate arrangements; we may make many mistakes from our own incompetence to judge; we may forget, in our objections, the capability of improvement which belongs to all human plans; and we may not see the difficulties with which the subject has to contend.

FELLENBERG'S VIEWS.

FELLENBERG'S VIEWS.

In the preceding remarks we have taken a view of the history of education and society in Europe, according to the impressions which reading and reflection have made upon ourselves. We have at the same time faithfully described the effect which the revolutionary spirit of the age had upon the mind of Fellenberg in his younger days, and the practical conclusions which he drew from it with respect to the necessity of an education of a totally different kind from any which previously prevailed in Europe, embracing in its operations every class of society in its peculiar wants, and extending to the whole nature of man, physical, moral, and intellectual.

In the following chapter we shall permit him to speak for himself: we shall collect his own expressions and trains of thought, as put forth on different occasions, as far as difference of languages will enable us to do so. We shall merely give them a unity and arrangement which they do not possess in the original, in consequence of their having been written at different times, and addressed to different persons, sometimes orally, sometimes in writing. The words of the original we shall generally preserve, and its spirit always.

We establish our institutions (says Fellenberg) upon the basis of Christianity; we begin our labours with the Gospel; we proceed upon its principles and conditions. Every sound system of education must begin and end with the instructions and lessons of Jesus Christ; it must rest on him and his doctrines, motives, rules, and principles. As his motives are the only ones upon which human character can be properly formed, so his revelations of its ultimate destiny and prospects are the only object of moral perfection to which it can be worthily directed; and the Divine assistance he has revealed and promised is the grand co-operation, without which it would be vain to indulge any hope of success. In the instructions of Jesus Christ is to be found the substance of the theory of education—the best practical example for the educator to follow; and in the result we should aim at no other object than the realisation of the kingdom of God upon earth, to which he has directed mankind.

The great traits of the character of Christ may at the commencement seem to our pupils like the first dawning of the rays of the morning, which are scattered and almost lost in the clearness of an unclouded horizon. The mind of the child is far from being able to comprehend the divine love of Christ, embracing all mankind with inexhaustible and profound sympathy; or his unbounded love for our race, and his intense labours and sufferings as a proof of his love. We cannot at first follow out this grand picture in all its details; we must begin with its principal features, and allow them to sink into the mind, to take root, to be well and familiarly pondered over; to become incorporated with the mind, and to appear natural to it and a part of itself, before we proceed to fill up the outline. We must wait till the mind opens more and more—till its faculties of judgment and reason, as well as its feelings, are developed. This advance of the mind must be watched, and fed as it proceeds and is able to bear stronger food. The system of Jesus Christ, though adapted to persons of all ages in its different departments, is yet to be worthily comprehended only by adult minds, and by those who have given all their energies to its cultivation: it is so comprehensive and sublime, that we may go farther, and say that every generation will find new views and prospects in it, as their own minds and intellects are more and more expanded and filled with all divine and natural knowledge. The essential points will not alter; but new beauties will come into sight, and an effulgence unknown to former times will burst upon the eye. We are none of us competent at present to understand all the mysteries of Christ: to us and to our children do they belong; and they will be revealed to those who come after us, in proportion to the fitness of their hearts and minds to receive them. These things we must remember in the instruction of children. This instruction is to be carried through a long succession of years; from the cradle to manhood; from the age of three or four, when they first begin to lisp their hymns and letters, through the period of childhood, up to that period when they can understand the reasonableness of the rule, " to whom much is given, from him much will be required:" and the prudence of the maxim, " keep your loins girded, and your lamps burning:" and the justice of the award, " thou in thy lifetime receivedst thy good things, and likewise Lazarus evil things; but now he is comforted, and thou art tormented:" and the awful truth and principle of human conduct, " if they hear not Moses and the prophets, neither will they be persuaded though one rose from the dead."

It is evident that these truths form a gradative system, adapted to the different ages of life; that they must be taught; and not merely taught by rote, but by feeling and conviction, to the opening, the growing, and the mature mind. What is suitable for the man is not suited to the youth; what is intelligible to the youth is not so to the child; but if the child has not been taught to feel and to believe the truth of the pathetic histories of the Bible during his age of young and vivid feeling, and to sympathise *with* all the good, and *against* all the evil, of which he hears from a loved parent's lips, he will never give a moral attention to, nor feel a moral interest in, the higher principles which will afterwards be displayed to him; nor discover a moral taste for truth as truth, when his mind is old enough and strong enough to appreciate the profoundness and importance of that question, "What is truth?"* Christ then, as a model, is to be continually held up by the educator to the eye of his pupils, from the junior to the senior class, as the bright exemplar and illustrator of human conduct, both in civil and religious matters, till at last they are able to receive him religiously as their head and Saviour, and the great head of the spiritual world. When they are able to attain to this view, the business of the educator may in a manner be said to cease, and to be handed on to the minister of religion. The two offices are in a degree blended together, and yet distinct; and it is a matter of delicacy and refinement to draw the line between them. For this purpose, the aid of the minister must be sought, and his specific place assigned in the business of education.

Never could the sublime morality of Revelation, and the exalted character of Christ, be better presented to the imitation and adoration of our race, than at this moment. Never could his example in instructing the ignorant, directing the wandering, and in delivering the world from moral evil, be more strongly recommended to the true philanthropist,

* See Note A at the end of the volume.

who may lay claim to the high office of being his true disciple. Our own age, like others, has its moral evils to encounter; those of a corrupt and selfish heart, of a proud and conceited scepticism, of dangerous theories and innovations, and of awful and sweeping revolutions. The human mind has received a wondrous intellectual enlightenment, mighty for good or for evil, with which our educators have not kept pace in their moral training. A new race of educators is demanded, who shall base all their classical and natural knowledge upon that rock alone where the waves of moral ruin cannot reach it,—the Rock of Ages, the Rock of Revelation, as a system of practical morals, upon the rock of Christ and of God. The study of the classics, of Greek and Roman history, will encircle the mind with subjects for comparison and illustration. Mixed up with an absurd and dangerous mythology, they contain models of pure composition and style, with profound remarks upon the principles of human nature, as they appeared to men of acute minds, who were unaided by the indispensable light of Revelation for a correct understanding of our nature: but at every step the pupil requires to have their beauties and errors carefully separated and pointed out, and their morality strongly contrasted with the only true standard—that of the Gospel. He may then perceive the infinite superiority of Christianity over the superstitions of the ancients, and the philosophy of their wisest men.

He will see the necessity of a Revelation for the moral wants and security of mankind, and be prepared for a full and complete course of Scripture history, so as to have a clear view of the most beautiful and harmonious of all subjects of contemplation—the rise, progress, and completion of God's miraculous dealings with men; the small and imperceptible beginnings by which he made himself known to Abraham, and convinced him, in an idolatrous age, that there was a God who made and governed the world, and would one day judge it; the more public and awful proofs which he gave of his government in the history of Moses; the race of prophets which he raised up, whose sublime compositions extinguish, in their superior blaze, even the idolised productions of Greece and Rome; the retributive history of the destinies of the Jews, as interwoven with that of other nations,—their prosperous virtues, their ruinous crimes; and lastly, the consummation of all, in the indescribable simplicity and sublimity of the religion of Christ—the poorest, meanest, humblest of mankind, and yet the most affectionate, pathetic, and profound of all; the servant of all, and yet the king and ruler of all; cut off in the flower of his youth, only to live for ever, both in the heaven of heavens and in the hearts and lives of men to the latest generations; and more near to each generation in proportion as it is more remote from the period of his death, because each generation, by its moral improvement, is more capable of receiving and appreciating the character of Jesus Christ, and, to use a strong figurative expression, of receiving him into their hearts; and because it is nearer to the day of his second coming to judge and to save.

This scheme, and system, and history of Revelation, leads at once to a practical result. It sets aside in an instant all inferior motives and rules in morals; it enters into no calculations even of the utility and advantage of virtue; it lays no schemes for attracting the applause of the world, or for securing a niche in the temple of Fame; its maxim is simple, persuasive, and overpowering, viz. " to do the will of God from the heart," and thus to "know that the doctrine is of God." Its most convincing argument is a life of purity; the weakness of man, the power of God. A pagan moralist imagines he can do all things, and ends by doing nothing,— he cannot even conquer himself; the Christian moralist, diffident of his own power to keep the least portion of the law, ends by keeping all in the power of another.

Thus, the best preparation for understanding and valuing the Christian revelation is to implant its spirit in the heart of the pupil, and to accustom him to act it out in his daily avocations, studies, and pursuits. Precept alone is meagre, dull, and dead; it is what is called " mere morality." The child must be accustomed to the exercise of benevolent *feelings* as a daily occupation, before he can understand the assurance that "it is more blessed to give than to receive;" he must make many unsuccessful efforts to walk steadily in the course of duty and prudence, before he can be convinced of his need of Divine aid and guidance, or before he can understand and feel the command, "If any man lack wisdom, let him ask of God, who giveth liberally, and upbraideth not." The young pupil must never be allowed to consider religion and religious sentiments as things distinct and separate from his ordinary life; instruction and practice, theory and action, must go hand in hand together. This habit must begin to be formed from the commencement; the pupil must be accustomed, with conscientious care, in every part of his intercourse with others, "to do unto others as he would they should do unto him," even in the most minute details of action and self-restraint; otherwise he will not be able, at any future period, to regulate his conduct by this fundamental rule without the greatest difficulty. From this early neglect of practice, and resting in the inculcation of mere precept, arise the constant imperfections which we see in the conduct of persons anxious to do what is right; and of which none are more sensible than they themselves, when they have once begun to study their own heart, and to act upon the profound, though pagan principle, "Know thyself."

This view of religion is the principle, rule, and practice of our establishment; but in addition to this, in order to do full justice to the pupil and the subject, and to give a sanction to its paramount importance, each pupil is placed under the especial care of a minister of religion, chosen or approved of by his parents, whose duty it is to instruct him, more deeply than school-exercises allow of, in the essential doctrines of Christianity. Thus, he is instructed in the faith of his parents and family, with as much care and earnestness as if he were under the domestic roof, while he is led, by the peculiar discipline of the school, to carry out the preceptive part into daily action and practical habits; at least, this, if not fully effected, is the aim and scope of the whole system.

The summary of this part of the education is therefore the following:—the whole of the Scripture history read, with portions committed to memory; selected books and divisions read critically, and committed to memory; a summary of Christian doctrines and duties, expressed as much as possible in Scripture language. In the upper classes, a more enlarged compendium of the same; a course of what is called natural religion and morals, according to the views which we are now enabled to take of them from the light of Revelation; the study of the Greek Testament; and finally, a concise and general account of ecclesiastical history. The religious services of the Sunday are intended both for devotion and instruction; and two lessons in the week are especially devoted to an account of the instructions of the preceding Sunday, in which explanations are given of any thing which was imperfectly understood.

It need not be said, that great difficulties sometimes arise on this subject with new pupils. They come at all ages, and from all kinds of previous training and instruction. Many have been sent hither as a last resource, when the character had been neglected or contaminated. Great consideration is requisite whether they can be received without danger to the other pupils; and if received, in what way their minds and dispositions may most judiciously be drawn into the studies of the place; how their barren thoughts may be fertilised, and their habits of indolence and self-indulgence exchanged for those of active duty and application. They are treated with great tenderness and consideration, as persons whose previous circumstances require pity and sympathy; they are made to understand the system and objects of the place, before a regular routine of study and employment is required of them; their better feelings, their ideas of propriety, and their good sense, are appealed to, in order to carry conviction to their hearts of the friendly and beneficial intentions and tendency of things around them. If these representations are found insufficient, after a certain period, to solicit their approbation and concurrence, and their previous habits appear irradicable, it seems wiser to allow them to return to their friends, than to prolong a useless and dangerous contest. But generally, the happiest consequences result from this considerate mode of presenting the subject. It is that which the divine Author of Christianity himself proposes for our model and imitation. Considering the almighty power which he wielded, it is wonderful how little recourse he had to threatenings, and how unceasingly he urged the language of persuasion; "Come unto me, all ye that labour and are heavy laden; take my yoke upon you, for I am meek and lowly of heart; and ye shall find rest." When he foresaw the calamitous fate of Jerusalem, though he knew he had to pass through the most bitter agonies from the cruelty of the people, yet, instead of any degree of satisfaction at the retaliation they were to undergo from the arm of another, he wept over their miseries, occasioned by their obstinacy and crimes. Such must be the general spirit of every system which would reform, establish, and perfect the human heart. Severity may occasionally be necessary, especially in those systems of which it is the principal feature, and in those schools which, like an army, can only be held together by corporal punishment; but in a system which lays any claim to the title of Christian, mild appeals to good feeling and good sense must form the rule of government, and severity must be the exception. We are of opinion that the present low state of morals in countries professing so pure, refined, and holy a religion as that of Christianity, is chiefly owing to the neglect of these grand principles of the Gospel in the education of youth; to their not being made the principal object in education; to their being postponed to the cultivation of mere intellect, without any mixture, or with very little mixture, of the heart and affections; the latter being made the exception rather than the rule. Perhaps we are to consider this fact as a proof that the minds of men are still very far removed from the spirit of the Gospel, notwithstanding the length of time during which religious establishments have existed, and the myriads of religious volumes which have been written. But to return: it is therefore the object of this establishment to build up education upon the Gospel — upon practical Christianity; to form from this the spirit of the school, of the teachers, and of the pupils; to consider the cultivation of the intellect as secondary and subordinate, and as springing out of the other as its root.

CONSCIENCE AND MORALS.

Having fixed upon the Bible as our basis of action — as the only basis of all human action — we have next to consider what man himself is, and in what way the educator, as far as human means are concerned, must proceed to draw out the feelings and faculties of the pupil towards the principles of the Bible, and to instil its spirit into his heart, so as to make it the motive and safeguard of his conduct. It is evident that to make the Bible useful, we must consider the nature of the being to whom it is addressed. Unless he had a nature corresponding to the instructions of the Bible, it would be perfectly useless to him. The Author of the one is also the Author of the other, and has made the two to answer to each other. We must therefore seek for the application of the one in the nature, principles, and constitution of the other. These must be studied as well as the book, if we would know how to apply the wisdom of the book, and to make it efficacious. We must assume that, as man is addressed as a responsible and rational being, he possesses a moral nature, a conscience, and an understanding: he possesses a will in common only with other animals; but he possesses distinctively, as man, a conscience, and an intelligent, reasoning mind. These two principles must always be kept in view by the educator. The will, which constitutes the final point upon which character turns, is assailed by an infinity of motives, which urge it to decide and to yield itself to their influence; whilst conscience and reason stand by, as it were, in awful suspense, to deliver in their verdict when the irrevocable step is made. How are these motives to be presented or controlled by the educator, so as to lead and fix the will to prefer what is good, noble, and Christian, to what is evil, low, animal, and ruinous?

The religious feelings are bound up with our very first impressions, if properly managed. The first conceptions and impressions of the infant are derived from the countenances and actions of those around him. The office and look of maternal love, and tenderness of maternal affection, open heaven to the child, through the medium of the heart of the mother. The maternal care which watches and labours for the good of the child with the warmest affection, the most anxious foresight, and the most unwearied efforts, without expecting any other reward than the delight of contributing to his welfare —which sees and provides for all that his mind can grasp—should give the child his first conceptions of the all-wise, all-good, and all-powerful God. Our first ideas of the character of the Deity, and of his infinite perfections, are derived from the manners, conduct, and affections of those around us, by separating the more perfect from the less perfect, and by compounding the former together into a simple whole. Therefore, if nothing which is good and amiable is exhibited to us by our first instructors, we can form no conception of a superior Being, who is all goodness and benevolence. There will be many drawbacks in the mind of the child, owing to the many imperfections of those about him, even in the best of characters; but if no virtues, or scarcely any, are presented to him—if the surrounding characters are vicious and inconsistent —the child will have no good position to start from, no rock to build upon; his experience will be a struggle amid conflicting experience and principles; he will hear and see occasionally what is right, and he will find an echo to this in his own breast; but he will see much more which is wrong, which contradicts the former, and will find in himself desires and motives at war with his other principles, without any overruling standard to refer to for decision. Thus good and evil hold a balance before him, in which the evil side predominates and the mind, wanting a decided preponderance and permanent ascendancy of right, is thrown upon its immediate gratifications, which are all of a selfish nature, according to the first law of a sentient being, which must be its own preservation and immediate enjoyment.

In our situation as educators and teachers, the most sacred duties of parents devolve upon us; we should therefore seek to present to our pupils the same disinterested, benevolent, unvarying, and consistent care, which they would receive from devoted and conscientious parents, with hearts willing to do their duty, and minds capable of doing it, in order that they may draw from us their first ideas of the Divine attributes and providence. In this view, our office becomes one of the most high and holy ones which men are capable of discharging, as the pupils have to receive from us the great principles of right and wrong, of a useful or pernicious life, of happiness or misery, of weal or woe, for time and eternity. Let no one think that our arrangements for this high purpose are too complicated and careful, too minute, too scrupulous, embracing too many objects of pursuit, study, or employment. We have the whole character to form, from childhood to manhood, and from the cottage to the palace, since we embrace in our system the education of every rank in the community. Without attempting to enfeeble with words what cannot be fully expressed, we must observe, that every appearance of nature which exhibits the wisdom, goodness, and power of the Creator, with the aid of a faithful conducting hand, will bring the child continually nearer to the invisible Creator, Preserver, and Benefactor, and lead him gradually to perceive his delightful and glorious relation to the Most High,—

> To look through nature up to nature's God.

For as the Bible is the will of God expressed in words, nature is his will expressed in actions.

Favourable moments should be seized, without forcing the attention of the child from the subject before him, to lead him to reflect on the superiority of the works of nature, considered as those of God, over all the works of man, in their beauty and perfection, and in their display of skill and wisdom; and especially in the powers by which the physical changes of nature are carried on, so totally unlike and superior to any power which man has hitherto been able to employ. The utmost power which man can employ is mechanical, and that belonging to the lower standard of mechanism; for its higher standards, as electricity, he has been unable to wield, for his own purposes, to any great extent. Besides these, nature employs as a superaddition a variety of vital energies, far beyond the control and conception of man, giving rise at once to the idea of a spiritual Cause, whose powers and resources are peculiar, distinctive, and incomprehensible. Thus the mind, properly led to observe and comment upon these interesting and extraordinary facts, is daily filling itself with the idea of Divine power, as shewn in his works, made visible and tangible at first, as if for the purpose of mathematical demonstration, but spiritualised by the studious and devout mind into an essence invisible and untangible like itself, and capable of making all things out of nothing.

Conscience is at first only a principle, having different degrees of original strength in different individuals, but capable in all persons of education and expansion, and of taking cognizance of all the actions and thoughts of the heart. It must be specifically cultivated, in order to be improved and developed. Most systems of education pay strenuous attention to the cultivation of the memory from the very cradle, as if they thought that all excellence were numerical, and consisted in the mere number of ideas, without regard to their nature or their relations and combinations; and by these means pupils may be brought to learn by heart with rapid facility many hundreds of words, without attaching any meaning to them. If we wish the conscience to be perfected, we must cultivate it with the same assiduity. We must first awaken it, and enable it to feel its own power. We must exercise it by constant appeals to it under all the circumstances which arise through the day. As there are no actions which do not bear directly or indirectly upon morals and conscience, so we must be constantly pointing out this relation. Conscience puts us immediately in connexion with the Deity himself. It is the principle in our constitution which enables us to feel his character as a moral Governor: mere reason would not do that. It requires a moral nature in us; and that moral nature is expressed in one word, CONSCIENCE, or in Scripture language, the HEART. But not only all the actions of the day afford occasions for an appeal to the conscience and the exercise of its peculiar powers, but the greater part of the reading of schools, which consists of history, poetry, and didactic works, affords the same; in them we exercise the conscience freely and without bias on the actions of others, and thus form it to a right tone of feeling and judgment. Thus there are two moral worlds, the inner one and the outer one, which, when properly taken advantage of, give as ample a scope for the cultivation of the powers of conscience, as the various books which are studied in schools do for the cultivation of the memory; and all this exercise ought to be so conducted as to lead us up to God himself as the superintendent and guardian and judge of conscience. It is something to have been created a being possessing this faculty; but the mere possession of it sinks into insignificance when compared with the sublime and all-important truth, that God is the guardian of it, and of its rights and responsibilities. The most unnatural thing a man could do, if he were responsible to none but himself, would be to act against his conscience; but now, having God for its guardian, it is also the most dangerous thing he can do, for upon it, and upon it alone, depends his eternal happiness or misery. It is therefore of the utmost consequence to begin early in life, even from the cradle, to awaken, call forth, and exercise this faculty—to obey its dictates as the paramount rule of life—to observe with wonder and adoration the infinitely kind, wise, and powerful hand, which, while it leaves the will free and responsible, yet teaches, instructs, and warns us, by the various events of life, to cherish and obey conscience, and through that to attain to the highest and purest joys of which our nature is susceptible.

The nature of right and wrong, the beauty of the one, the hatefulness of the other, can never be learned by a child as abstract truths. Without the relations of man with man, the moral law not only has no application, but cannot even be fully comprehended. We become accessible to the voice of the law which regulates our intercourse with our fellow-men only so far as they appear before us. They may be presented to us either in the commerce of life, or by means of historical and biographical descriptions. Without such points of comparison, we have no means of forming a just estimate of individual character; and it is not until we have observed and considered the actions and characters of many of the most noble and excellent men, that we are capable of forming any thing like a just estimate of the resplendent moral glory of the Saviour.

The world of little children in which the pupil lives and acts is the first, the most natural field for his observation. Intercourse with those of his own age is more useful for the excitement and development of his mind, than with adults. The continual watchfulness which should observe all their movements will discover constant opportunities to present living examples of abstract truths. Every occasion of this kind should be taken advantage of, and the child should be thus taught to refer his actions, and those of his companions, to a superior law or rule, and to understand the meaning and importance of the law by a continual application of it to his conduct.

REMARKS

ON THE PRECEDING ACCOUNT OF

FELLENBERG'S

RELIGIOUS AND MORAL VIEWS.

THE preceding observations on the subject of religion and revelation are made, as we have said, as much as possible in the words of Fellenberg. We have attempted to give a faithful transcript of the mind, feelings, and object of the author, in order that his views and labours may be fairly and fully appreciated. The more these are examined and understood, the more highly must this venerable character rise in our estimation, and the more important must his labours appear to the welfare of society at large, because of the practical nature of his institution. He has devoted his life and fortune to the attempt to bring down religion from heaven to dwell among men, to adapt the theories of religion to common life, and to embody during the weekdays those truths which are spiritualised on the Sabbath. All this was in the mind of Fellenberg half a century ago. At a time when the learned and refined world of Europe considered revelation as at best but a beautiful fable, Fellenberg both felt and acknowledged its truth, and conceived the illustrious idea of forming a practical system of education for all ranks, based upon the reception of its precepts and the authority of its laws. He did this both theoretically and practically: theoretically, as considering revelation to be a message from the Almighty of incalculable importance; and practically, as considering an improved system of moral and Christian education to be the only remedy for human vice, depravity, and revolutionary fury; as well as the only preventative of the future repetition of those awful scenes which were then acting in Europe, desolating her fairest provinces, and sweeping whole classes of society, of the highest order, from the face of the earth.

We have now further to consider and to detail the various means by which he proposed to carry these ideas into effect.

PRACTICAL DETAILS.

FELLENBERG purchased about two hundred acres of land, of which fifty were arable, for the scene of his experiments. His views comprehended the improvement of the agriculture of his country, as well as that of the character of the inhabitants. He intended to make the cultivation of his own estate the model by which others might learn how to improve theirs. The improvement was to consist in drainage and irrigation; in manuring and mixing soils; in the rotation of crops, and in introducing new plants for cultivation; in the perfection of old instruments of agriculture, and the invention of new ones. He had a passionate fondness for agriculture, and great ingenuity, invention, and skill in the mechanical arts. He therefore established workshops upon the estate, in which all the implements of husbandry for his own use, and for general sale, were fabricated; including also a department for making and preserving models of all machines in use, or which it was proposed to bring into use at any future time. The plan embraced a better arrangement and construction of the farming buildings, and an improved method of managing the cattle. All, in fact, that had been done in England during the last half century, for the general improvement of agriculture, by various societies, was aimed at by Fellenberg by himself alone, in reference to the capabilities of his own estate and country. But Fellenberg's views and principles led him to perceive what in England had not been thought of—the bearing which the pursuits of agriculture might have upon the morals of mankind. Daily labour in the open air is the most healthy of all occupations, both to the body and mind. Children who are brought up in the country acquire, under ordinary circumstances, a hardy constitution, which is denied to the children of towns. Perceiving that labour might be regulated and modified so as to become a system of moral instruction, as well as one of industrial employment, Fellenberg determined to convert a portion of his estate to this purpose, and to make an agricultural school his first step towards the moral training of children, and the improvement of their character. Peculiar as were his ideas as to the proper methods to be pursued, he could derive no assistance from others in the commencement; nor could he collect together a sufficient number of children from their parents who might be induced to remain with him long enough to give his plans a fair trial. His first school, therefore, was formed of the destitute or abandoned children of the neighbourhood, partly, no doubt, from necessity; for, till confidence in his views had been established, no others were to be had. But Fellenberg was prompted in this by other motives also; by a deep and religious conviction that the Deity had, in the energetic language of the apostle, originally made " all men of one common blood;" that the lowest, as well as the highest, are born with the same susceptibilities; that the vices, therefore, into which the lowest ranks sink, are engrafted by their position, and the neglect of their superiors, and might be prevented by early care, or obviated by better culture. The feelings of society, he found, were against these conclusions; and he felt the obligation of a Christian pressing upon his conscience to remove such debasing and unfounded prejudices. To rescue the poor from their moral degradation thenceforth governed all his views. He considered that the destitute children whom he might collect, and who commonly became the pests of the community, and the objects against whom the penal laws were generally directed, would prove at once a test of the truth of his own principles of education, and of the real causes of the degradation of their character. His agricultural school was therefore his first essay in education.

AGRICULTURAL SCHOOL.

The success of a school of this kind depends entirely upon the master, who must be not merely the teacher of reading and writing, but the companion, friend, guide, and parent of the pupils: he must never quit them, by night nor by day; he must take his meals with them, labour with them, rest with them, explain every thing to them, instruct them, play with them, and sleep in the same chamber. Without such a master, whom the children can love, because he is kind and amiable,—reverence, because he is of a certain age and character,—and respect, because he possesses a fund of knowledge and information useful to them on all occasions, and to which their curiosity can always apply and be satisfied, the system cannot succeed. Fellenberg was himself the friend and instructor at the beginning; but it was some time before he could meet with one to supply his place in a character at all times perhaps difficult, but then entirely new. At last he discovered in

Vehrli, one of his pupils, the disposition, kindness, simplicity, judgment, tact, and knowledge, he required. This person entered completely into his views, perceived their extensive and beneficial nature, and felt the honour of assisting in so valuable and useful an institution. He acquired the practical facility of conducting it, and did so with entire success until he removed to a school of his own a few years ago. The following are the details of management :*

The children rise in the morning at half-past

---

* Children should be admitted at the age of five or six years, and remain in the institution till they are twenty-one. During the first ten years they are an expense to it: during the last five years they repay, by their labour, all the previous outlay upon their education. They then obtain situations in the world—in agriculture, or in some mechanical art, and maintain themselves like other workmen, by their skill and industry; but being better taught and superior workmen, they more readily find employment; and being of a better moral character, they fill places of more trust and emolument; and possessing habits of greater economy and prudence, they turn their earnings to better account.

In the year 1813, twenty-six years ago, a commission was appointed to visit and examine the agricultural school at Hofwyl. At the head of it was Reuyer, one of the most distinguished men in Switzerland. They spent six days in examining all its details —food, dress, accommodations, religious exercises, studies, labours, and occupations. It then consisted of twenty-three children, taken from the lowest classes, the highways and hedges, destitute and abandoned; they were now living in harmony, peace, and affection: punishment was seldom wanted; when necessary, it consisted of mild rebuke, remonstrance, in four or half-past five o'clock, according to their age. Half an hour is allowed for washing, dressing, making their beds, and arranging their rooms. They *then* go to prayers; *then* to lessons, for one hour in summer, and an hour and a half in winter, and *then* to breakfast; *then* the master allots to each class, or to each individual, his employment for the day. At eleven o'clock they dine, and *then* have a lesson of an hour or an hour and a half. At four or five o'clock, according to the season, they have bread given them, and a third lesson. At seven o'clock they sup, and the master reviews the work of the day, and the conduct of the children. Their beha-

private, or in public before the other children; exclusion from social meals; and lastly, corporal, which, when necessary, is inflicted with the greatest consideration and concern, so that the pupil may perceive that nothing but necessity could have extorted it from the teacher. This necessity is explained to him; the danger, degradation of character, and ultimate misery and ruin occasioned by crime, and the propriety of preventing refractory habits by bodily pain, when higher and moral motives are insufficient. Corporal punishment is never required except for new pupils.

One evening, after an interesting lecture, Vehrli cautioned one of the children, without mentioning his name, to be on his guard against a fault he had committed; immediately all became serious and silent, each seeming to take the reproof to himself. Very often, when conscious of having committed a fault, they pass judgment on themselves, and absent themselves from meals; Vehrli then sends them their food to a private room. In the year 1832 this school consisted of one hundred boys.

viour and character are particularly noticed: praise or blame are bestowed according to circumstances; and the motives, principles, and responsibilities of human conduct, are explained and illustrated from what has happened among themselves, as far as is suitable, and intelligible to their understandings. They then have prayers, and the youngest go to bed, while the older ones amuse themselves in any way they please—with reading or gymnastics, but generally with music, in which they delight, and which is made to serve a most useful purpose in softening their hearts and characters. The children of the Swiss peasantry are continually exposed to all weathers, and therefore become hardy and robust, and remarkably free from diseases; the children of the agricultural school are brought up upon the same plan: they wear no hats, and in summer-time no shoes; their clothing is simple, clean, and comfortable; their bed a straw mattress. They assist in preparing their own food, which is the same as that of the peasantry—soup at every meal, vegetables, bread and milk. They eat meat only once or twice a-week; and on holydays they are allowed the wine of the country. The children are habitually cheerful, happy, and healthy, which is a sufficient proof of their being properly fed and clothed.

During the summer they spend more time in working on the farm than in winter; but their employment is adapted to the age and strength of each child. The youngest are occupied in picking and breaking stones, or in weeding. During harvest, ten or twelve hours are employed on the farm, and only between three and four in instruction. In the winter the school-hours are six or seven.

When the weather does not permit them to go abroad, they learn to make baskets, and various useful works in straw, &c. They are all taught to mend their own clothes.

In order to teach habits of order and carefulness, each child has a special office assigned to him: one keeps the chambers clean, another the furniture, another the pavement, &c. Three of them are chosen to superintend and inspect the whole, and are changed every three months, in order to accustom them to all kinds of work and duty. Even the youngest have some office found for them.

They are allowed to work for their own profit. Each child has a garden of his own, which he cultivates with flowers or vegetables; he collects all his manure from the roads, or from the dead leaves of autumn; he either sends the produce to market, or sells it to the establishment, when he is allowed its value at the end of the year, with interest, even upon so small a sum as a franc. Two or three children will go shares in a garden or a fruit-tree, and dispose of the produce in the same manner. The elder ones constantly assist the younger ones in managing their ground. A principle of order, method, and the division of labour, pervades all the details of the establishment. The management of the farm is a distinct office by itself. The master of the children, though he works with them, has nothing to do with the accounts of the farm; he merely works with the children, under the superintendence of the bailiff, that his whole attention may be devoted to the behaviour and studies of the children. For some years, in the infancy of the establishment, when the number of children was small, Vehrli was able to superintend all the children himself, and to study and influence all their characters: this became impossible when the number of the children increased. Vehrli then acted as general director, and under him assistants were placed; and it was found that fifteen or eighteen children were the greatest number who could be effectively superintended by one assistant. At the same time, Vehrli continued to watch over the whole, and to hold a private conversation with each pupil at least once in the week, and so to retain their affection and esteem. When the masters were thus increased in number, they held private occasional meetings, in which the general principles and objects of the institution were explained, observations and suggestions made by each, and the conduct and management of the pupils detailed; difficulties were stated, and their remedies proposed.

The first assistants were not easily found; but as the establishment proceeded, promising pupils were selected, who were prepared for the future office. These went through a wider course of instruction than the rest, and were allowed the advantage of being taught in the higher school, which was formed by Fellenberg about the same time. Here they were also employed as the teachers of the junior classes of the higher school, filling the double office of teaching and being taught alternately. This plan has been found to succeed beyond expectation: the improvement in knowledge and manners, among those of the agricultural school who have studied and taught in the upper school, has been greater than any one had been sanguine enough to expect.

The agricultural pupils are distributed into classes, both in their sleeping-rooms and their labour, according to age, capacity, and character. A pupil of doubtful or bad character is placed among those whose characters are confirmed and good, who exercise over him a salutary influence, according to the great law of sympathy, example, and the force of numbers and of opinion.

The youngest classes, besides the inspector, who never quits them, have a selected pupil placed over them, who acts the part of an elder brother, overlooking and protecting them, and taking care that they keep their persons and dress at all times clean.

The discipline of the agricultural school is mild and simple, like that of the other schools. It is based upon religion, and addresses itself to the conscience and the understanding, and not to fear. Its greatest reward is the pleasure and happiness of doing what is right; the greatest praise it meets with is the sentiment of approbation. The constant superintendence under which a pupil is placed prevents his persevering in a fault: if he repeats it, he is reprimanded; if it be of sufficient importance, it is reported to the superintendent. A reiterated fault is reprimanded more severely; and if that is not enough to prevent it, the pupil is separated for a time from his companions. Corporal punishment is rarely inflicted: when it is so, and is still ineffectual, the pupil is expelled, as being incorrigible, and too dangerous a companion for the rest. This case rarely occurs; and when it does, it is among new-comers. The religious principle, with mild expostulation, generally produces a reform.

Fellenberg considers the great art of a rational and methodical education to consist in finding active and useful employment for every moment of the day. Children are not able to do this for themselves—it must be done for them; and whoever does it is the true and only educator. It must be done under a direction; and then there is no time for idle, useless, frivolous, or mischievous employment, nor even for bad thoughts. All must be innocence where all is useful and agreeable, and where, by an incessant vigilance and inspection, nothing objectionable can be done, heard, nor seen. Thus vice is prevented from entering the school: it has not to be cured and driven out when it has taken root, for it is not allowed to gain admission. This is no difficulty under proper arrangements, like those of Fellenberg, because, the children being happy, and interested in their pursuits, desire no other: all their faculties are gratified; their curiosity, their desire of knowing the properties and uses of all surrounding objects; their taste for nature, which all men are born with; their taste for music and drawing, which are also common to all; and their desire for active employment, which is also universal in childhood. All the educator has to do is to direct these tastes and desires to useful purposes, and to shut out the approach of evil, and of all counteracting objects and occupations. The system is very simple when once carried out into practice, as has been done by Fellenberg; so that it is a wonder mankind have not discovered and adopted it before.

This agricultural school affords the best model of education, not only for the children of paupers, but for those of all the peasantry. Their path in life is rendered simple, by their being furnished with the means of happiness; every envious and hateful feeling is extinguished by the spirit of Christianity, and by the value they are accustomed to set upon a good conscience. All useless instruction is avoided; yet no knowledge is despised or neglected which may hereafter become necessary. A knowledge of, and skill in, agriculture, by which they are to get their living, is made the means of cultivating their understanding, and of forming their heart and character.

The system might be imitated in all countries, upon the principle which Fellenberg has discovered, viz. that the earnings of the pupils from the age of fifteen to twenty-one are sufficient to repay the previous outlay. The expenses of Hofwyl are not entirely repaid, because the benevolence of Fellenberg induces him to receive the children of the peasantry without any engagement for them to remain till they are twenty-one, and many of them are removed before that age, and before they have received the full benefit of the system; but a sufficient number have remained to enable a general estimate of expense to be made.

If such a school were established in another country, some of the difficulties which Fellenberg had to encounter might be avoided, and the expenses diminished, and the success of it rendered more complete. Fellenberg in the commencement could, as we have seen, use no selection in his children; he took the destitute and the orphan under his care, without any regard to their individual disposition and character. He seems to have done so partly, as we have already allowed, from necessity, but partly, perhaps, to prove more clearly the truth of his system and principles: as if he had said, " You take the best children, and bring them up in your way; I will take the worst, and bring them up in my way; and mine shall turn out better workmen, better subjects, and better Christians, than yours." If he had made such a challenge, he would have won the prize; as it is, he has proved his point, which is, that the making the working classes good workmen, subjects, and Christians, is a matter of choice, and may be effected any day, as soon as the upper classes, or a certain number of them, wish it to be so, and attempt to carry their wishes into effect by the means he has pointed out.

Fellenberg considers that every man is born with the most valuable of all capital—the sum-total of his faculties of body and mind. But this capital is worth nothing till it is cultivated and employed; and the cultivation consists in what alone makes his capital profitable and productive—the education of the labourer. If this capital be brought out and educated, it becomes national wealth; if neglected, the labourer becomes a burden, by consuming more than he produces, and by becoming a destructive criminal. The capital of the labourer's possible skill and industry is like that of a mine, or the soil,—though ever so rich, it yields nothing till it is worked. One of the products of this capital is self-happiness; and the happiness of every man depends upon the skill with which this innate capital, with which he is born, is worked. The truth is universal, and applies to all ranks of life—*Memoria nihil est nisi eam exerceas.* The best natural abilities, which ought to constitute the happiness of the person and family to which they belong, are lost or perverted for want of education, or by an injudicious one. The amount of national benefit which would be derived from a well-trained peasantry may be calculated numerically, as we calculate the amount of its crime. This calculation would far exceed the most sanguine views which have hitherto been taken of the improvement of man. When the moral improvement of the labourer shall have become a general object of pursuit, upon the principles now proved to be practically possible, we shall have invented a moral railroad, by which the great ends of morality, religion, and national wealth, will be reached with as much speed and certainty as commercial purposes are accomplished by physical railroads.

The peasantry who have been educated in the agricultural school of Fellenberg may be distinguished from others who have not been so educated, by a kindly spirit, and a quiet, peaceable conduct, which never forsakes them. They are always ready, in the Christian spirit, to help and assist others; and have no desire to quit their station in society, but are perfectly contented with their condition in life.

If similar institutions should be attempted in other countries, and children should be admitted above five years of age, as at ten or fifteen, and still kept till twenty-one, the expense of the establishment would be less, but the formation of character would also be less perfect. Those who are educated by the common methods, or who are not educated at all, must necessarily possess a character more or less vicious, at whatever age they are selected to be placed in such a school; and this character, if not incurably bad, would take long to reform, and prove a serious injury to the institution. Such an institution, if unsuccessful, would be no argument against the agricultural system of Fellenberg, though in proportion to its success it would confirm his views. Those establishments in England called "refuges" are under great disadvantages. They take children of a certain age, who are hardened in crime; who have been educated in crime; who have been rejected by society, and become outcasts on account of their crimes; who have thus, as it were, been interdicted the use of earth and water, in being fit for no honest means of earning their daily bread,—who have never been taught any. Yet even these have been found capable of some reform, —willing to learn a trade, willing to work, sensible to kindness, grateful for it, open to religious impressions, and thankful for religious instruction. Had such children been placed under wholesome instruction and training when infants, and continued so till twenty-one, it is impossible not to believe that they would have been, in all respects, useful and religious characters. The persons who have undertaken these institutions, under all their disadvantages, must possess the highest and purest principles of our nature, great enlightenment of understanding,—great faith in the stability of the principles of man, in his moral and rational powers, when properly cultivated,—and, above all, a profound sentiment of the character of

God as viewed in its holiness, justice, and immutable rectitude, and love for his offspring. To believe that God is indifferent or opposed to the happiness and perfection of man, is one thing; to believe that he will promote that happiness and perfection only through the use of means properly sought out and applied, is another and a totally different position. He may delay the discovery of those means for ages, as he has done some of the most useful and valuable discoveries in art and science; but as the means have been at length discovered of attaining great perfection in the one, we have a right to conclude, by a strict logical analogy, that they will be discovered in the other. Besides, we are not left even to analogy; we have a more sure word of prophecy, that is, of Scripture: for no one can be much in the Bible without seeing that all its preceptive morality is prophetic of a moral kingdom, at some future time to exist on earth, in which all arts and sciences shall co-operate to one great moral end, the Christian regeneration of the world. Revelation would be almost futile without it.

Some such hopes and principles must have filled and animated the bosoms of those persons — call them philanthropists, call them Christians, call them people of common feeling and common sense elevated into a principle — who in this country, in the midst of many discouragements, both in the undertaking itself, and also in the low and unfavourable state of public opinion on the subject, could risk their credit and good name, could draw upon themselves the responsibilities of the undertaking, could expose themselves to the ridicule and odium of party-interest, could compromise even their worldly prosperity, for the sake of exploring a new path of duty, which, though promising much in anticipation, was necessarily beset with piercing thorns in its commencement:

> Illis robur et æs triplex
> Circa pectus erat.

MEYKIRCH.

WHEN Fellenberg had proved experimentally the truth of his ideas by the success of his agricultural school, he proceeded to prove it still more decidedly by the colony of Meykirch, six miles from Hofwyl. In the year 1816 he purchased fifteen acres of woodland. Thither he sent a master with about twelve children. They were to build themselves a house, to clear and cultivate the land, and to employ their leisure time in learning to read and write, and the elements of knowledge. They were supplied with tools and materials from Hofwyl, and with food till they could raise enough for subsistence. In seven years they repaid all the expenses of their outlay, which was about 150*l.*, and maintained themselves upon their little territory. Fellenberg calculates that fifteen acres of land would support a colony of thirty children upon this plan, which is the greatest number suited to such a system; and that it might be established upon land not available for the general purposes of cultivation. The only difficulty is, to obtain a superintendent properly qualified by temper, character, religious principles, and a complete knowledge of details.

This colony was compared very naturally to the story of Crusoe upon the desert island. It drew all its supplies at first from Hofwyl, as Crusoe did his from the ship. The children were delighted at the comparison, and worked at their enterprise with the greatest alacrity and zeal, and became naturally strongly attached to the cottage reared by their own hands, and the land converted from a waste to a garden by their own labour. When these little emigrants arrived at the spot which was to be their future home, they found nothing but a shed on the side of a precipitous mountain, under which they slept upon straw covered with sail-cloth. They had to level the ground, and with the earth and rock to form a terrace in front, which soon became a garden. The cottage they built was of one story, with a basement which became the kitchen and dairy, which occupied together twenty-five feet in front. Above this was one room, about twelve feet wide, for the day-room, behind which was a dormitory of the same size, and behind this a stable of the same length, and about nine feet wide. An open gallery was in front of the day-room. At each end of the building was a shed about fifteen feet wide, and running back upon a level with the stable. So that the whole front of the building was fifty feet, and the depth thirty-three; and it was finished in about two years. The colony subsists upon milk, potatoes, and bread. Three hours a-day are devoted to instruction, the rest to labour accompanied by explanations. The same system is pursued as at Hofwyl:—reading, writing, drawing, singing, natural history, the history and geography of their country, common arithmetic, mental arithmetic, geometry, land-measuring; a portion of botany, so far as relates to agriculture; the nature of soils and manures, and the rotation of crops; platting, sewing, spinning, weaving; social prayer night and morning, religious conversations, Bible lessons; the feelings and affections roused into action in the midst of their tasks; the duties of life pointed out, as depending upon their relation to one another and to their heavenly Father, his universal love to his creatures, and the inexpressible glories of his works. In the prayers which the master and pupils offer up morning and evening, they never omit to refer to the advantages and blessings which they enjoy in this asylum, nor to pray that all orphans and destitute children, in all the world, may every where find kind protectors who may establish similar asylums for instructing and educating them, so that they may become good Christians and useful members of society.

This colony is one of the most affecting sights in the world. To behold the happy results of youthful labour, the intelligence of the children, and their contented and grateful dispositions, living upon a fare which most people would despise, and eating nothing but the produce of their own exertions, having converted a wilderness into a garden, and made the desert to blossom as a rose.

When Meykirch was first established, they wanted water. To attain it, they were obliged, under the direction of a skilful workman, to excavate a passage into a sandstone rock five feet in height and 280 in length.

On Sundays they attend the service at the chapel of Meykirch, and very frequently at Hofwyl.

An establishment like Meykirch possesses one very great advantage, peculiar to itself, over a large one like that at Hofwyl, which is, that the pupils see the whole fruit of their labours constantly under their eyes. The house they live in, the fields they cultivate, the food they eat, the clothes they wear, are all the produce of their own hands. It is strictly and properly their own. If any articles are brought from other places, they are bought in exchange for their own productions. But in a large establishment this sense of personal production is lost sight of in the multitude of producers, and the ramifications and changes of the produce. We cannot help thinking that there was a period in European history, when the wants of the peasants were supplied very much by domestic manufacture, and when the state of society resembled a good deal that of Meykirch; the children were brought up under the eye of the parent, and engaged in some kind of domestic labour, spinning, or knitting, &c., till they were old enough to go to field-labour. The contamination of towns had not reached the country, and the manners were more pure. If it ever were so, that state of society has passed away, never to return; and the benefits of it upon the character of the young must now be sought for by more artificial methods — by an enlightened and Christian philanthropy anticipating evil habits by a precautionary system, and applying the best improvements of modern art, science, and moral management, to the judicious formation of habits of intelligent labour — in agricultural schools formed after the successful model of Fellenberg.

"Agriculture," says Fellenberg, "seems to be peculiarly fitted by Providence for the education of poor, necessitous children. When taught systematically and intelligently, it excites the faculties of observation and reasoning, even among those who learn it only to live by it; but the particular end which an enlightened benevolence proposes to itself will only be fulfilled in proportion as we teach the pupils to delight in assisting and obliging their companions while they are working on their own account. At Meykirch, the pupils are so situated as to perceive that these two objects, the personal and common good, go hand in hand together. If new pupils arrive, their assistance is felt to be useful in completing the common asylum. Their pleasures and enjoyments are in common: industry and Christian feeling are promoted by the same means, and travel together in perfect harmony. Is it going too far to say, that that prayer, ' thy kingdom come, thy will be done on earth,' is here fulfilled?" Destitute and abandoned children, who would otherwise perish as outcasts, here become Christians, and earn their subsistence contentedly, cheerfully, and gratefully. It is in nature, the grand laboratory of the Creator, which is now put in harmony with the Gospel, that we must seek for the means and elements of primary instruction and education. Our utmost wishes may be accomplished by placing the rising generation under the care of well-trained instructors, in the midst of nature, safe from the contamination and corruption of the dense and neglected population of towns, which cannot grow up otherwise than vicious.

"When the pupils of Meykirch were made acquainted with the miserable state of Greece, and the multitudes of children which became destitute in consequence, they made a collection of what they could spare for their relief, and petitioned in their prayers that they might meet with the same education and protection which they themselves possessed.

"It must not be supposed," says Fellenberg, "that education consists in removing difficulties from the path of the pupils; it consists rather in teaching them how to surmount them. They must be taught to conquer both external and internal difficulties: to overcome the first by steady labour, well directed; and to master the second, viz. their own passions, by habitual self-command. No occupation is so fitted for this purpose as agriculture, provided it be followed under a kind, judicious, and religious guide, who may direct and moderate the efforts of the pupils, which are sometimes apt to run into excess, as at others they would sink into idleness and disorder."

Some years ago, the river Linth overflowed its banks, and converted a considerable tract of country into a useless marsh. An eminent engineer succeeded in draining this by a canal; and it was proposed to establish upon the reclaimed land a colony of poor children, upon the plan of Meykirch. The plan happily succeeded; and while in progress, the children at Meykirch took a lively interest in it, made a collection for it, and offered up prayers for its prosperity.

Should similar establishments be formed in other countries, either for the education of destitute children, or for the reform of criminal ones, like the refuges of England, Fellenberg recommends that the latter should vary in the strictness of their discipline and inspection, according to the character of the children sent to them. In proportion as these are more vicious and hardened, their labour should be more severe, their discipline more rigid, and the food, though wholesome, yet coarser; and that the moral inspection should be more minute and searching, and moral and religious instruction more studiously impressed. Thus, the mind might be subdued through the body, and labour and temperance might pave the way to the subjugation of the passions and appetites.

When the agricultural school was fully established, Fellenberg formed one for girls, upon a similar industrial plan, as far as the nature of female occupations permitted. All kinds of female industry formed the chief employment, and mental instruction was introduced as secondary and subservient to the former. The school was under the immediate care of Madame F. and her daughters. The object was to form good domestic or farming servants, or good managers and housewives for the peasantry; at the same time that attention to mental cultivation, which consisted in practical moral principles, a knowledge of the Bible, and the adoption of its spirit as the practical guide of life, was made a leading object, as in the boys' school.

We may take this opportunity of observing, that an industrial education in these days is totally different from what it was, or could have been, a century ago. It would then have been mere labour without mental exertion, and without principles either moral or religious: that seems to have been the character of many of the old charity-schools; the children were kept to constant labour, like animals, in unwholesome apartments, and upon a bad diet, without any mental instruction whatever; they were consequently cramped in mind and body; the masters frequently abused their office, and overworked and ill-treated the children. The present day-schools, which attend merely to mental instruction, however imperfect in forming character, are still far superior to the old charity-schools. But the enlightened labour-school of Fellenberg gives to labour a moral character; and the instruction with which the labour is accompanied, and the intelligence and kindness of the superintendent, give to the same name a totally different meaning. In this school the children, even if they were never to learn to read, would become more intelligent, and better qualified for service, than most of those who are now educated in our best national schools; they would have a practical knowledge of an extensive kind. Agriculture taught in this way comprises in itself a vast fund of knowledge, and all of it of importance: soils, geology, mineralogy, drainage, land-measuring, manuring, chemistry; plants, vegetables, forest-trees, fruit-trees, botany; implements, machines; animals, for labour or for food — their habits, food, management, — are but a few of the particulars.

In Fellenberg's school the knowledge is chiefly communicated to the children by word of mouth, not from books.

The secret of the system lies with the educator.

THE HIGHER SCHOOL.

FELLENBERG would not have done justice to his comprehensive views and wishes, had he rested in his agricultural school. He conceived that the characters of all classes depended upon the habits and principles imbibed in their education. The elementary faculties and principles of human nature are the same in all ages and in all classes. The character of the grown-up man depends upon the age in which he lives, the class in which he is born, and the education he has received in that class, —comprehending in that word not only his book-instruction, but the moral training, and the companions with which he has been trained, or those with whom he has associated. Peculiarities will arise in the intermixture of these principles, which may appear at first sight exceptions to general laws; but they will be found, on examination, only to be branches of higher laws, and not to be by any means aberrations. Thus, the good sense, judgment, vigilance, intelligence, and piety of particular parents, may keep their children from contamination, and habituate them to right discipline from the cradle to the age when they are too old, and too enlightened, and too strongly confirmed in good principles, to be corrupted. Till the world becomes more moral and more Christian, this parental vigilance and good sense is perhaps our best hope for character; but in the present state of the world it is of rare occurrence. Sometimes it seems to fail altogether, and the best parents, or those who seem to be so, have unprincipled and profligate children. But in these cases it will generally be found, that though the parents had some of the points of good educators, they had not all. In this case the moral argument is like the mathematical one — some of the necessary data are present, others are absent. Can we wonder that the experiment does not succeed? It is impossible it should succeed. Nature is consistent and logical; she will bend to no one's caprice; she is stern, inexorable, and unflinching in her laws; she pities the weakness and blindness of her children, but she will not forgive them. Let no man hope to be unscathed in that warfare, in opposing the moral laws of nature.

Again, an individual may be born with a rare combination of principles. He may possess the higher faculties strong, the lower ones weak. He may have a clear and strong conscience, a good judgment, an energetic will, a paramount sense of right and justice, with unconquerable firmness; the lower appetites may be moderate or weak, they may require but little self-control, while he possesses it in abundance. The temptation, therefore, to do wrong is small; the inducements to do right are many and strong. Such characters exist from birth. Genius extends itself to morality, as well as to works of intellect and fancy. Some men are born great moralists, as others are born great poets, mathematicians, musicians, or mechanics. These are practical points of the utmost importance. They have never been studied by educators, nor even by metaphysicians. The moral children should be searched out, and well instructed, and be selected for the instructors and educators of others. Such characters will persevere in virtue, or goodness, or religion, call it what you will, in spite of all obstacles, and come out of the fiery ordeal of life victorious over all temptations.

These considerations are not to lead us away from the general law or fact, that the character of the mass of mankind is formed by circumstances. Upon this principle Fellenberg proposed to establish a school for the higher classes, in which the usual branches of a first-rate education should be taught by the best masters; but the school should differ from others in the following respects:—

1. The subjects taught should not be confined to a knowledge of Greek and Latin, but should comprehend the elements of all subjects which are useful in the conduct of life,—modern languages, natural philosophy, natural history.

2. The number of teachers should be increased, so that the teaching of each should be more complete, perfect, and satisfactory, by having fewer subjects and fewer pupils to attend to.

3. No one subject should be considered as intrinsically superior to another, but each should be important in its place; and its relative importance should only be estimated like the objects of nature, in which nothing is predominant, and nothing can be spared. The whole would be imperfect without the presence of all the subordinate parts; and all are important in their place, and in the conception and plan of the great Architect.

4. In giving this general education to all the pupils, there would still be room for making distinctions

according to the taste and genius of individuals. When the individual taste was clearly declared for languages, or natural philosophy, or pure mathematics, or natural history, he could have the opportunity of indulging that taste, in consequence of the abundant supply of masters or professors who were obtained to reside in the establishment.

5. It was not an object of the school to be a nursery for other institutions, where excellence in some one acquisition was held to be the criterion of all human excellence. When this is the object of a private seminary, as in most English schools, all studies must be sacrificed to the one in which all excellence is supposed to consist. Thus, a particular species of composition used to be thought the perfection of the human mind. Now composition is properly the order and arrangement of knowledge in a perspicuous method; but scholastically it was nothing more than stringing words together according to certain arbitrary rules, and had no reference to the sense and the subject-matter. Thus nonsense-verses were once an important part of school-exercises; and at all times it would be difficult to conceive how boys could learn to arrange knowledge when they had none to arrange. However, Fellenberg avoided this difficulty, by discarding the idea that the acquisition of a prize constituted human perfection.

Fellenberg's school has been improperly compared with other schools, as if success in getting prizes constituted the criterion of its merits. This was unjust to him, who never professed such an object. It might as well be imputed as a fault in the Gospel that it did not make scholarship its test of excellence. Fellenberg determined to be a Gospel-schoolmaster, or none at all; to make his pupils men of principle, while he enlightened their minds, and to leave prizes and academic honours to those who valued them.

A great question has been raised in Europe of late years as to the methods of teaching Latin and Greek. We spend ten years in learning these languages, and 1500*l.* of money, and at last we know them very imperfectly; therefore, say the public, the method is bad. No, say the teachers; you are idle and stupid. Then, say the public, since we are too stupid to learn the dead languages, teach us something useful. No, say the teachers; we teach this or nothing. But Fellenberg says, " excellence in languages is like other excellence,—it depends upon individuals when the foundation is laid. Those who are properly taught will afterwards become proficients, if they have the taste and inclination; those who have no taste will never learn, under any system. But if they learn not the dead languages at ordinary schools, they learn nothing. But we will give them the opportunity of learning, not merely the dead languages, which they may have no taste for, but that without which they are unfit for life, and which they may have a natural taste for life, if not for " the dead languages."

6. And again; " we wish to form our school, not upon a system of prizes, but upon a system of character. We wish to teach our pupils in what excellence really consists, and not to mislead them with false views and erroneous estimates of human duty and responsibility. We do not teach them that excellence consists in any one acquisition whatever, but in the harmony of all, and chiefly in the use made of every acquisition. What we labour at, is not the quantity acquired, but the relative value of it, and the use made of it."

Far be it also from Fellenberg to sit in judgment upon the particular use and application of old and national institutions. He is not a MEDDLER; he does not condemn, or pull down; he assists, and builds up; he had no wish that his institutions should spread before they were tried and found successful. He had no wish to supplant old institutions, but to form new ones, to serve as remedies for evils notoriously and widely existing. The scholastic subjects and methods of instruction might serve the purpose of education for a particular system of society, while it left untouched a considerable portion of evil which infested a collateral part of that system; and till a remedy was found out for the collateral part, the machinery of the other part might continue. But Fellenberg had no such system to support; his was not a part of that scholastic system; and he might therefore be well excused in entering upon a new field, which, without interfering with any other, would supply certain wants which were widely felt and complained of.

"There is a large class of young men," says Fellenberg, "who are men of property and influence in different parts of Europe. They are sent to the present schools, because there are no others. They do not want a knowledge of the dead languages, nor do they want college-prizes. Prizes are no distinction to them; they are distinguished by their hereditary renown. What they want, is the general, not the scholastic, cultivation of their mind. They want the elements of scientific, interesting, useful knowledge; not of philology or school-logic. Above all, they want the cultivation of the heart, which the schools never taught. They want to know that they have a heart, a conscience, and an eternal responsibility; that their birth, rank, and wealth, are but a responsibility, on which the happiness of thousands, perhaps of millions, depends even in this life, and for which they will have to account to their Creator and Judge in the life to come. To teach this is my business; but to teach it is not the work of an hour, but of a life. A precept or a sermon will not effect it; it requires a whole youth of training. They must be trained, not lectured. This, therefore, is the principle of my school,—to form the character. It is nothing to say, that my pupils cannot carry off prizes at Paris, Vienna, Berlin, Oxford, or Cambridge. I train them not for that, but to return to their families in peace, as affectionate sons, intelligent masters, vigorous in manly constitution, benevolent to their inferiors, loyal to their kings, upright in all their transactions. These are the objects which I propose to myself. By them I must be judged, not by academical honours. I wish to form men apt and fit to exercise all the arts and honours of peace or war, as Milton has so well expressed it."

Thus Fellenberg began his school for the higher classes; and as it was not a preparatory school for any higher seminary, but one which professed to finish the education of those who frequented it; and as he believed it to be desirable to form the mind by means of a circle of sciences or studies, he was obliged to imitate a university in introducing a complete universal course of languages, sciences, history, literature, drawing, music, &c. Still, the acquisition of knowledge was made secondary to that of a good healthy constitution of body, and of firm moral and religious principles. He had obtained the secret of producing these effects in his agricultural school; and by a judicious and discriminating modification of these means to the higher school, he succeeded in his object in that also. The number of hours devoted to study in the higher school was increased, but they were fewer than in ordinary schools; while the occupations of the pupils between the hours of study were so systematised, and arranged, and superintended, that no time was really idly spent; nor had the pupils the opportunity of acquiring objectionable habits. Gardening, agriculture, and gymnastic exercises, fill up the intervals between school-hours. A practical knowledge of agriculture, and of the construction of machines and implements, form a great subject of study, both on account of its healthiness, and because many of the pupils are heirs to large domains, in which their knowledge may be turned to the best account.

The same preventive system of inspection prevails in both schools. The boys are not allowed to acquire vicious habits, and then lectured upon their sinfulness; but the formation of the habit is prevented by ever-watchful vigilance; just as the eye of the parent is ever awake, in the early years of life, to prevent those numberless accidents and improprieties to which the inexperience, as much as the wilfulness, of children is liable.

But this preventive system is not incompatible with the fullest enjoyment of the boys. The inspector is present to prevent mischief and vice, not to check the sallies of youthful joyance. The inspector is the friend, not the "*pædagogus acer*," of the school. He is ever ready to explain, instruct, and to compose any differences which may arise, and never loses sight of the one grand principle of human life, that all men are brethren, tied to each other by different degrees of consanguinity, and that the happiness and well-being of the whole is made up of those of each of the individuals.

The arrangements for the night are made upon the same principle. About twelve pupils sleep in one room; but when they retire to rest they are accompanied by an inspector, who does not quit the room till all are asleep. It is impressed upon their minds that the night belongs exclusively to repose and sleep. As soon as the wants of the body are supplied, bed becomes relaxing and enervating both to body and mind. The pupils are therefore habituated to fall asleep as soon as they go to bed, and to arise at an early hour, as soon as they awake. The great secret of obtaining sleep is exercise in the open air, inducing bodily fatigue. It was long ago observed, that "the sleep of the labouring man is sweet, whether he eat little or much; but the abundance of the rich will not suffer him to sleep." Thus the principles of a good education have been known to the wise for ages; it may almost be said that Fellenberg alone has reduced them to practice.

The relation between the highest and lowest classes of society has formed a subject of great dispute and uncertainty. Some have considered them as totally opposed to and incompatible with each other; that wealth and rank on the one hand imply poverty and misery on the other; that in a perfect state of society, all should be equal. Some, who approve of a distinction of classes, imagine that it is so far unnatural, that while it exists the lower classes must be degraded, discontented, and unhappy; that consequently there always must be in them a latent spirit of insubordination and dissatisfaction, which can only be kept quiet by force in the higher classes acting upon ignorance in the lower ones.

Fellenberg considers the distinction of ranks to be a natural law of man, and a providential appointment of the highest and most benevolent wisdom. It provides for every kind of pursuit, occupation, and study. It brings all the faculties of body and mind to their highest perfection. Universal perfection may in a degree belong to mankind as a race, but it cannot possibly belong to man as an individual. The acquirement of one physical excellence is necessarily incompatible with that of its opposite; so of the qualities of the mind. To bring to perfection all the bodily powers, a number of persons must be trained, each in his own department. Much more is this principle requisite in mental pursuits, which are infinitely more varied and incompatible than those of the body.

The idea that the lower orders of society are naturally discontented, and envious of the higher classes, has arisen from this cause, among others, viz. that the upper classes, and the schools in which they are trained, have hitherto too much inculcated the principle of rivalry and an insatiable ambition. They have done all they could to spur on this principle.

From the very cradle, taunting and invidious comparisons are made; personal superiority is fostered and lauded for its own sake, as possessing an intrinsic value; rivalries and jealousies are encouraged and fomented. No independent rule of right and excellence is established. All excellence is resolved in a great measure into this, that it consists in some personal superiority over another. The inferior person is always more or less degraded.

Those who have been brought up upon this principle imagine, that to be beneath another in rank or wealth is to be degraded, miserable, and discontented; and therefore that the lowest class of society must necessarily possess these feelings, and be at constant enmity with the higher classes. Nothing can be more unphilosophical than this notion, or more repugnant to our conceptions of a wise Providence, or to the truths of revelation. The rivalry-spirit is one which belongs essentially to a barbarous state of society, not to one of Christian civilisation. The savage provokes every other savage to a jealous rivalry, while the Christian provokes his neighbour to love and good works. The rivalry of schools is one of the legacies of savage life, in which all happiness was deemed to consist in personal superiority.

Fellenberg, relying on his conviction that the distinction of classes is a Divine appointment, considers that the better the two classes of high and low understand each other's real position and circumstances, the less will the lower one be disposed to envy the higher one, and the more will the latter be inclined to respect and sympathise with the former. He therefore formed the two schools near each other, as parts of the same establishment. The pursuits and occupations of both were carried on in sight of each other. The higher pupils could observe that the lower ones had the same affections and faculties as themselves, and were as full of happiness and enjoyment, while their labour was absolutely necessary for the comfort of all; that in the midst of this labour they were contented and cheerful, free from envious passions, and imbued with sentiments of respect and attachment for their superiors in rank; that their minds were equally capable of cultivation, as far as their leisure-time allowed; and that they were as capable of receiving pleasure from the beauties of nature and of art. Above all, they could see that they possessed the high principles of morality, and justice, and the love of truth, equally with themselves; that they were as incapable of falsehood and hypocrisy, and possessed hearts as bold, true, and loyal, as belonged to the best of the land.

On the other hand, the agricultural pupils perceived that the condition of the higher pupils was not one of idleness nor of unmixed delight; that they were subject to a discipline as strict as their own, though of a different kind; that each hour brought its allotted task, which could not be omitted; that during the hours of leisure and exercise, the enjoyments of each seemed to be equal; that occasionally it was evident that the other pupils had secret causes of dissatisfaction peculiar to themselves; that a more luxurious mode of living did not appear to be accompanied with more pleasure than a more temperate one; and that the expenses of the higher school were a source of immediate profit and advantage to themselves.

Thus, in happiness and enjoyments the two classes appeared to be equal; while in the production and distribution of the produce of labour, they appeared mutually essential to each other's comfort; the labour of the one being necessary on the one hand, and the capital of the other on the other hand.

Fellenberg's system allowed of an explanation of this mutual relationship, and afforded him the opportunity of inculcating lessons of kindness and good offices among the higher pupils toward the lower ones. Presents were occasionally made to them, and assistance afforded, either in the purchase of useful tools, &c., or in times of sickness; and the same charitable spirit was called forth towards the parents of the children who lived near, and towards the other peasants of the neighbourhood. Thus the end of Fellenberg was attained in the higher school; which was, not to produce great scholars or men of abstract science, but good men for every-day life, who might feel and acknowledge the brotherhood of all mankind, and promote, to the utmost of their power, the welfare of the community.

VILLAGE SCHOOLMASTERS.

When Fellenberg had succeeded in his three schools, he began to think how the blessings of the agricultural school might be conveyed to the villages of his country where it was most wanted. For this purpose, he selected the boys who were most fitted for the purpose, and trained them for masters instead of workmen. When they quitted the establishment, they returned to their native villages to act as common schoolmasters, and to train the children under their care, as much as possible, upon the principles of Fellenberg, *i. e.* to form their character upon moral and religious grounds, and not merely to teach reading and writing as barren arts.

Fellenberg also invited the village schoolmasters from all parts of Switzerland to spend their summer vacation (which lasts nearly three months, on account of the peculiar summer-occupation of the peasantry and their children,) at Hofwyl, at his own expense, that they might study the details of the establishment, and particularly of the agricultural school. Every part of the system was explained to them; and lectures were delivered, both explanatory of it, and also of those subjects which might be useful to them in their ordinary profession.

The subjects more particularly attended to in instructing the village schoolmasters are—1. Religion; 2. the language of the country, in reading, analysis, understanding the subject read, the expression of the thoughts by writing or in conversation; 3. arithmetic; 4. writing; 5. drawing; 6. music. To these are added occasionally the most useful parts of natural history, anatomy, natural philosophy, geography, history of Switzerland, outlines of general history, history of Christianity. The instruction is partly by books, partly by the oral teaching of the professor.

Though all these subjects are taught, yet the higher object of the heart and understanding, and the inculcation of good principles, are kept steadily and principally in view throughout. Fellenberg meets his pupils every evening, to review the work of the day, to encourage their efforts, to impress upon them the importance of order, neatness, and exactness in their own schools, of a discipline at once mild and firm, and the advantage of extending their influence, if possible, beyond the school-hours of the children, to their private pursuits and domestic conduct.

The last days of their stay are devoted to a general examination of all that has been done, by the professors, and in the presence of deputies from the government of Berne. The last day is dedicated to a general fête, to which all the inhabitants of Hofwyl are invited; and on the following morning the teachers return home, each with his knapsack on his back, grateful for the generous hospitality they have received, and anxious to turn to good account their new talents among their native villages.

INTERMEDIATE SCHOOL.

ONE more institution was necessary in order to complete the circle of Fellenberg's benevolent and judicious ideas. He had now successfully established his model-farm with its workshops, his agricultural school for the poor, and his high school for the rich and noble: there wanted an intermediate school for the children of the middle classes, in which the usual branches of education might be taught at a moderate expense. The system of this school was to be less laborious and more intellectual than that of the agricultural school, and less intellectual and comprehensive than that of the high school.

The great value of agricultural labour having been sufficiently proved, in forming the physical constitution and in influencing the moral character, and even the healthy condition of the intellect, a modified system of manual employment in the open air was introduced into this school; and whatever the employment was, it was made the subject of explanation and instruction, as in the agricultural school.

Thus, in Fellenberg's system, no time spent in the open air is lost for the purposes of instruction, as it is in most schools. The business of the teacher is not over when the school is closed: he is still teaching by oral explanation and observation amid the work or even the games of the children. His book is then the great book of nature, " whose minister and interpreter" he is, to use the language of Bacon. He is then surrounded by an infinity of objects which strike the senses with palpable lessons, instead of the dry, arbitrary characters of books, which too often convey no instruction at all.

RECAPITULATION.

HAVING thus presented a view of the history of Fellenberg's mind upon this important subject; of his feelings of benevolence towards the destitute, and the vicious and criminal; of his motives and religious principles; and of his machinery for attaining the object of his wishes, viz. an improved moral education and character, and improved intellectual abilities — we will here present those means at one view.

1. A model-farm of the most approved methods of cultivation.

2. An experimental portion, about one-tenth of the whole, for testing new ideas, new machinery, new plants, new methods of draining, manuring, ploughing, sawing, cutting, &c.

3. Extensive workshops for manufacturing agricultural implements, either for private use or public sale.

4. A workshop for the manufacture of model-machines, either of those in use, or of those imported from abroad, or of those proposed to be tried at some future period.

5. An agricultural school for the children of the

peasantry, whose chief employment is labour, under a well-informed teaching, either in the fields, garden, or workshops; and whose intervals of labour are employed in learning the elements of knowledge.

6. A school of industry for girls, upon the same plan, as far as difference of sex permits.

7. A provision for training masters for agricultural schools.

8. A summer school for the instruction of village schoolmasters.

9. An intermediate school for the education of children of the middle classes of society.

10. A high school for the education of the children of the wealthy and noble families.

CONCLUDING REFLECTIONS.

FELLENBERG has succeeded in what constitutes the highest efforts of a great genius, *i. e.* in the harmonious union of elements apparently, and at firs sight, heterogeneous and contradictory. He has united labour with learning; the acquisition of a trade or manual employment as a means of obtaining a livelihood, with the cultivation of the mind; all the advantages of country pursuits,—fields, forests, mountains, fresh air, exercise,—with all the advantages of towns—books, society, professors, lectures, arts and sciences; the contemporaneous education of the highest and lowest classes, each acquainted and sympathising with the other, knowing each other's character, pursuits, sources of happiness or anxiety, and yet not interfering with or incommoding each other, but, on the contrary, mutually benefiting, by the interchange of capital for the produce of industry, and by kindly offices, as in real life; the public education, whose principle is discipline and strictness, and the mutual influence exercised amongst numbers,—with the domestic training, whose principle is personal kindness, mildness, indulgence, and, when necessary, expostulation; the most vigorous and manly health of the body, with the highest cultivation of the mind; the education of the peasant, with that of the legislator, the politician, and the nobleman; the most gentlemanly manners, with manual employments of what would be thought a humble kind. He has made useful and laborious employments honourable, and directed honour into useful paths. He has shewn that agriculture, the most useful of all arts, is also the most moral and enlightening, and the most fitted for being made the basis of education, either for high or low; that as no pursuit is more calculated to prevent vicious habits, so none is more effectual in eradicating them. Sleep is the grand restorative of body and mind; it gives new vigour to the faculties, as well as to the body. Who does not know its effect in fixing an idea tenaciously in the memory? But it must be sound; and sound sleep is the result remarkably of some kind of agricultural labour in the open air. Cincinnatus was called from the plough to command the army and the senate. Enough use has not been made of this memorable fact: it includes the profoundest wisdom, applicable in all ages. Fellenberg has almost alone understood it, has acted upon it, has systematised the principle, and sent his young nobles from practical agriculture to cultivate, adorn, and rule their own domains, and grace the courts of their sovereigns by unsullied integrity and enlightened ability. He has perfected, at the same time, the mind and the body; he has also perfected conjointly the heart and the head; he has made religion predominant in the heart, and yet based the understanding upon principles,—a difficulty seldom overcome; for men are generally either superstitious or sceptical. A pupil at Hofwyl cannot be superstitious, for he is surrounded by facts; he cannot be sceptical, for he is surrounded by evidence. No sooner has he caught a feeling than it is fixed upon a principle, upon a law of nature, and upon the Lawgiver of nature. Even his doubts are valuable, for their solution becomes to him a moral demonstration. To doubt with an enlightened companion is to reason; to reason is to prove. The strongest doubt, clearly solved, leads to the firmest conviction. Feeling and conviction are the two ends of Fellenberg's lever. Uniting them, the human mind is at rest in principle, but ever progressing in knowledge, benevolence, happiness, and wisdom.

Fellenberg has made all his children, from the orphan to the noble, from the peasant to the professor, revolve round one common centre, that of religion; this is the secret of his influence. But he has drawn every one into activity; this is the secret of his success. To converse with him, you would suppose him an apostle; to visit his farm, workshops, schools, you would suppose him a man of business, a man of the world. On this account visitors to Hofwyl draw the most opposite conclusions from what they see, according to the time they stay, the parts of the establishment which they observe, or the conversations they hear. One thinks Fellenberg an enthusiast, another a speculator, another an interested proprietor,—because he has improved his property. To draw a fair conclusion upon a momentous subject, which is no less than the happiness of millions, and the peace of governments, and their protection from a demoralising and revolutionary spirit, which has been long abroad, and perhaps is not yet quelled,—every part of the establishment should be examined, with the motives and views of the owner, and an induction made upon a full collection of facts.

There is an analogy to this in nature. To look at the beautiful external world, we might mistake it for the Divinity himself: it was so mistaken in former ages. God is matter, said the ancient sceptic; and mind is matter, says the modern sceptic. To look into our own minds, and feel their spirituality, we might be tempted to conclude that spirit could not produce so opposite a substance as matter, and that matter is self-existent; so says scepticism in all ages. The fact is, that every part of the universe is so important, and so teems with wonder in itself, that while surveying it, we see not the necessity of any thing else, nor the connexion which binds together an infinity of wonders.

Forty years have elapsed since the foundation of this establishment: we are unable to say how many since its entire completion and success, in the formation of the intermediate school, the last stone of the edifice. But England has not yet sent a messenger to inquire the news and to report, " to bring the " grapes from the valley of Eshcol." Some few individuals have wandered so far, and have amused a small circle, on their return, with a partial detail of its phenomena, as they have done of the noble mountain-scenery in the neighbourhood. How few have understood the moral lesson! Three thousand children are annually committed in London as offensive criminals against the laws: they are annually punished, and again let loose upon society to live by crime. How few have inquired whether it be possible to reform them, and to make them useful members of society; and whether there be a spot in the world where such children are reformed, or are so trained as not to need reform! Yet it has been proved that these children might be reformed without expense; for they would repay, by their labour, all the expenses of the reform. Yet no one has been officially sent to inquire. Those to whom the guardianship of morals is committed have not inquired, How can crime be prevented, how can criminals be saved?

If it be allowable to love one's country instead of a party, it is to be hoped and prayed for, that some educator may soon arise, heaven-born, " to turn the hearts of the disobedient to the wisdom of the just,"—to locate himself with thirty orphans or destitute children upon fifteen acres of land, there to build for themselves a sacred home, a house of labour, and a house of prayer and thanksgiving; rearing around them the food they eat, and preparing the clothes they wear, or an equivalent for them; and setting an example to the neighbourhood of peaceful content, useful labour, religious principle, and social happiness. Or when shall the educator arise for the higher classes—for that great majority of them who wish not to be great scholars or mathematicians, but men of useful knowledge and common sense,—a knowledge which belongs to their own business and bosoms, which shall qualify them for the management of their estates, and for the improvement of those who live upon them, their tenantry and their peasantry?

This is now the consummation devoutly to be wished for. The effect of punishment, as an instrument of reforming the human mind, has been tried, and has failed. Prisons, hulks, transportation, death, have had their fair experiment. The invention of legislators and judges has had a full trial, and has effected almost nothing; and is only persevered in from a sense of overwhelming necessity. Let the invention of an English Fellenberg be now applied to, to do that by prevention which others have in vain attempted as a cure.

And yet there is no obstacle in the way of the educator when he shall appear. He has but to do his work and prosper. If he shall shew an example of an English Meykirch, men will see and believe; and some who see will go and do likewise. If the laws of England have provided no educator, neither have they forbidden one to be provided. He is in the moral world what a new machine is in the manufacturing world,—a desideratum. He will be received, when he appears, with open arms and with smiles, rather than with frowns. Let him only arise, and he will prosper. Such is our fervent wish and our increasing conviction. It is impossible that the success of Fellenberg can fall to the ground, or be lost upon England.

England deliberates before she acts. She collects her facts before she draws her conclusions. She may occasionally appear to sleep; but she is only then pondering, in order to choose, decide, and act. Her institutions for religion, charity, arts and sciences, cover the land, and are still increasing. When she has once caught the idea of moral institutions for the practical formation of character in early life, she will display the same sagacity, integrity, and ardour, in this humane, enlightened, and glorious march, as in all the other brilliant achievements of her history.

Crime and pauperism, the present great blots in her scutcheon, will diminish, and perhaps by degrees disappear; and she may then send forth with confidence her swarms of hardy, virtuous, and intelligent peasants and mechanics, to cultivate her numerous and vast colonies, carrying with them the religion, laws, arts and sciences of their forefathers, to people the wilderness, to make the desert blossom as the rose, and to gladden the valleys with industry and plenty.

Her language, religion, and national freedom, will spread to unknown lands; she will instruct and convert savage nations, and Christianise the heathen; and if, in the midst of her earthly glories, she maintains a humble, grateful, and devout spirit, rendering due honour and homage to Him who has honoured her, she may long continue a great instrument in the hands of a beneficent, but mysterious, and withal a retributive Providence, for civilising, enlightening, blessing, and perfecting mankind.

Note to p. 40.—The colony of Meykirch was put an end to in the latter part of the year 1835: the pupils returned to Hofwyl. Fellenberg was unable to purchase more waste land, which would have been requisite in order to continue and extend the colony. The object of the experiment had succeeded in proving the possibility of redeeming waste land, and making it pay its own expenses. The land was then let as a regular farm.

NOTE A.

THE following remarks on the subject of religion, drawn from various parts of Fellenberg's writings, appeared to be too great an interruption to the immediate object of the work to be introduced into the body of it; but as they could not be omitted with justice to his general character, and as they contribute to give it a finer polish and a deeper tone, they are here recorded.

The nature and law of the human mind is a law of birth and commencement—of a nascent, incipient being—a law of development and improvement—a law of continual progress, of indefinite and perhaps of infinite extent,—we therefore follow that law from the beginning, and make it, not only the basis of all instruction, but also its constant companion; testing, balancing, and supporting every thing; and appropriating every acquisition to its proper position and station.

There are two points, among others, to be considered in religion—the one is, the idea of a revelation itself; the other, that of the life and character of the Author of the Christian revelation, Jesus Christ. The first involves the idea of the want of it to man himself, considered as a moral agent, and with reference merely to his situation in this life. Man is said to be compounded of a low and a high nature—the one, which he has in common with the brutes, of an animal appetitive kind, continually urging him to the preservation of the body and of its grosser gratifications; the other enabling him to look upwards to art, science, intellect, right and wrong, and the world of mind and of spirit. The low nature comes first into exercise, anticipates in a measure the high one, and fixes all the habits against it, before the period of its action and influence. Hence, when the higher nature begins to operate in the mature man, and he awakes, as it were, from the dreams of youth and of imagination, to the realities and responsibilities of his moral being, he finds himself too often in a wilderness where he expected a paradise. His youth has too often been both mispent and badly spent; it has not only been negative as to good, but positive as to evil. During that period, habit, the law of our nature, has formed us in spite of ourselves, and brought us into wretchedness, from which we strive in vain to escape. We may say, in a certain sense, that without any fault of our own, but by the irresistible influence of the circumstances of our education, we find ourselves devoted to the lower part of our nature, and strangers to the higher part. Such would be the history of mankind, if left to their own natural faculties. They would never be able to rise above the animal part of their nature, nor above the savage state of society. If we observe some nations of antiquity, previous to all knowledge of a revelation, making some advances beyond this state of degradation, we must consider it as owing to the general arrangements and operations of Providence, with reference to an existing partial revelation, and an intended universal one. The ancients did not owe their progress, strictly speaking, to the force of their natural faculties, but to the secret and unknown superintendence which they received from an affectionate Providence, who had better things in store for his family of man, and was preparing the way for happier times and seasons.

As a further proof of this, we see that even in our day, with all the advantages we possess of knowledge and the diffusion of Bibles, yet all which has hitherto been accomplished by parents, nature, and conscience, in the education of children, has been inadequate to insure to them Christian minds and dispositions. We fail even with the Bible in our hands—what could we hope to do without it?

This is one view of the nature, value, and necessity for a revelation, viz. the impossibility of ever raising man above a savage state without it—above a life of sensual indulgence and gratification, into a moral and intellectual life, aspiring to improve and exalt his own character, and benevolently endeavouring to soothe the ills of suffering humanity, the afflictions and wants of those around him. Men would have no fellowship with men, without the principles of a revelation, but would live the life of tigers, with ingenuity added to their savage faculties to heighten their natural ferocity.

Another view of a revelation is, that without it we could never know what our nature is capable of, even n this life, much less in another. We could not know that this mind, so weak and feeble, so ignorant at its birth, so full of appetite and passion at a more advanced age, does yet possess within it a germ of immortality which cannot be destroyed nor separated from it, which may unfold itself, even in this life, into a character of high and consummate excellence. We are authorised by revelation, and by revelation alone, to pronounce upon the possible character of man, and to assert *that* as a certainty which would without it be considered only as a poetic dream. Indeed, the assertions of revelation respecting the future development of the human character, though they deal in certainty and fact, are more sublime and glorious than poetic imagination has ever yet been able to conceive,—not only more than it has dared to conceive, but more than it has been able to conceive. They fully justify the hopes and exertions of those, in modern times, who have been called, rather in derision, the Philanthropists, but who have been able to conceive and to appreciate this exalted view of the future human character which revelation declares will take place, and who have very consistently searched zealously and indefatigably for the means which, according to the principles of human nature and the ordinary dealings of Providence, are calculated to conduce to that end, among which an improved system of moral (including in that term religious) education is no doubt the most efficacious.

The other point of revelation, viz. the life and character of the Author of Christianity, is another subject of consideration for those who engage in the education of the young, with the hope of establishing their character upon a Christian basis. The divine Author of Christianity did not merely give the world a set of precepts of a superior moral tendency, and leave them to make their own impression upon it, but he lived a life of illustration; so that what he practised, rather than what he taught, contained the principles he wished to enforce. He desired his followers, and through them all mankind in all ages, to live as he lived, as well as to practise his precepts; for all his precepts were embodied in his life, and became practically explained and exhibited in it; so that had he said nothing in the way of precept, his principles and maxims would have become evident to the attentive student of his character, and intelligible to those who wished to become his disciples, and to follow him in the moral of his life.

We must remember as educators, that the whole Bible is a record of a similar principle, that is, an illustration of high human character by the example of many eminent men devoted to the entire sacrifice of SELF, in order to attain to that purity and dignity of nature which was intended for us by our great Creator. It is true that these men have intermixed many precepts with their own histories, and that many are also recorded unconnected with practical examples; but wherever they stand, they are illustrated, and made visible and intelligible, by the living examples which succeed each other, like characters in a drama, throughout the whole of the history. It is not a little remarkable that, with so many bright examples before us, we should at last have One so much brighter as to cast all the rest into the shade. One, not a citizen of a particular region, with a certain mannerism about him unsuited to another clime, but a citizen of the world, speaking and acting like ourselves, so as to appear almost to belong to our own age as much as to one of two thousand years ago. There is a natural simplicity and propriety about the precepts, and actions, and conduct of Jesus Christ, which seem to belong and to be suitable to every age and to every country. He is, in all respects, the perfect model of a perfect and faultless human being; a model which, on that account, as well as on many others, can never be hoped to be reached by any other person: but still its perfect naturalness and propriety render it most proper to be set before all ages and classes, as their model of excellence, which they are to study, to understand, and to imitate, as far as circumstances, and their own powers, and the will of God permit. This, then, is another point in which revelation is invaluable. It has given us a model of which we can say—Look at this, and imitate it; " go thou and do likewise ;" " look unto me, and be ye saved, all the ends of the earth." Here is a model and a prophecy— a rule and an example—a direction and an encouragement. From this we draw an unanswerable inference in favour of the future amelioration of the character of man on earth. It would have been trifling with human hearts, if so much precept, and so perfect an example, had been given us in vain. Had the improvement of man on this earth been an impossibility, had it not been contemplated in the order and intentions of Providence, all religious precept, history, and example, would have been thrown away ; it would have been little less than a mockery of poor human nature. No; the precept and history of the Bible looks to a future earthly reality ; and the model of Jesus Christ, though far above what man will ever reach, is nevertheless a type towards which he will be continually tending, while he is continually polishing off the deformities and roughnesses which render him as yet so infinitely inferior to his great original.

We may remark further, with respect to revelation in general, that it harmonises in the most perfect manner with the instructions which the Deity has already afforded us, in so many ways, in the sphere of what is called natural religion, concerning our highest good. It adds a full security to our faith, which would have no solid ground to rest upon, if left to itself without a higher sanction, considering its situation amid many difficulties, arising from the ignorance, scepticism, and vices of men. Revelation, in the midst of a world of selfishness, inculcates the most extensive and noblest benevolence, and the most active and disinterested philanthropy. It teaches, or rather commands us (for all its precepts are commands), to love, not only our natural friends, but our enemies also, those who may have sought our injury. It recommends this sentiment by actions as well as by words, in the exhibition of the life of its Founder, who spent his life in doing spontaneous and unrequited good to men of all parties and opinions and of all nations, knowing beforehand that some of these very persons would assist in putting him to death; and who crowned all his other philanthropy by voluntarily suffering a cruel death for the sake of shedding incalculable blessings upon all races of men through time and eternity. Without this love, philanthropy, and death, mankind would have been as much lost as the independence of a nation is whose armies are beaten in the field, and her capital in the hands of her enemies. Such would have been the lot of miserable man,— a prey to savage ferocity, ignorance, crime, and woe. Revelation comprises a moral law for the gradual improvement of man, which eighteen centuries have not only not been able to improve, but have not yet arrived at the perfect comprehension of; for when any modern philanthropist, after the example of Jesus Christ, conceives the possibility, and attempts to prove the practicability, of realising the moral code of Christ in the hearts of the young, by a more careful and judicious education, he has frequently been looked upon as a visionary enthusiast; according to which view Jesus Christ himself must have been a visionary enthusiast, and must have died in vain, when he contemplated the happiness, improvement, and salvation of man as the consequence of his death,—a supposition almost amounting to blasphemy. The moral code of this revelation penetrates the sanctuaries and inmost recesses of human nature, leaves neither depth nor height unexplored, and is adapted to the peculiarities of all periods of life, conditions, and nations. It has continued to advance and spread for eighteen hundred years, and to triumph over the prejudices and vices of men, notwithstanding the weakness and frailties of those to whom it was committed. It has maintained itself against all the attacks of its enemies; and through all these contests, as through a series of confirming and purifying trials, it has become at this period, what it will continue to be more and more, the highest glory of God the giver, and of man the receiver.

APPENDIX.

We here subjoin an abstract of the opinions and sentiments of Dr. C. H. Scheidler, professor of theology at Jena, on the subject of education in Europe, and of the establishment of Fellenberg. He calls his book, "The Vital Question of European Civilisation;" and he views the system as seriously connected with the present and future well-being of society in Europe.

"It appears to me necessary to make a few historical and political observations on the present critical condition of our civilisation. We behold two broad and striking facts, the increase of poverty in the lower classes of Europe, and of demoralisation in all. The disorganisation which exists to so great a degree in France and Spain, exists in a less degree in all Europe. The political horizon is gloomy: the continuance of peace seems doubtful. If a general war begins, no one can calculate its awful consequences amid a population at once so enlightened and demoralised. We ought therefore to seek for remedies in time; and if any probable ones are in existence, to apply them judiciously and boldly to our position. We must not be content with mere suggestions and proposals of improvement, since these would justly be deemed Utopian; but we must require practical experiments of many years' growth, such as may satisfy the minds of practical statesmen in these critical times.

"The visionary schemes for promoting the improvement of society which were proposed by St. Simon, Fourier in his Social Colonies, and Owen in his Labouring Communities, prove the morbid state of society, its passion for excitement, and its dislike of regular, steady application of body or mind, at the present moment.

"No improvements which relate only to the outward forms of society will reach the evil. Even an extended representative system, however good it may be in itself, is insufficient. These outward forms require an inward guarantee; for they may at any time be annihilated by a *coup d'état*. Improvement can only arise out of a respect for what now exists, endeavouring to modify and improve it, but not to supersede it.

"In every respect, the educational establishments at Hofwyl appear to answer the demands of the day. They point out, in a positive and practical manner, a radical cure for the corruptions of modern civilisation. They do not present us with imaginary proposals, but with substantial and accumulated facts, which have been tested by the experience of many years. They contain a whole, consisting of many parts, every one of which maintains its own proper and specific relation to the rest, and to the natural concerns and business of life.

"In order to understand them properly, we must go back to the period preceding their formation, and the attempts then made, by different individuals, to arrest the progress of social demoralisation.

"Rousseau was one of the first of modern geniuses who strongly pointed out the evils of modern society, the corruptions of the higher classes, the narrow pedantry of the learned, the universal attention paid to a dry intellectual culture, and the utter neglect of the heart and affections. His constitutional character, no doubt, led him into extremes; he took morbid views of life, and even considered all civilisation as an evil, and neglected too much the consideration of religion as an element of social progress. Still, his writings had great influence, particularly in Germany. Basedow, Campe, and Salzmann followed, who though they had great errors, yet opened a larger range for the education of the mind generally, particularly in the study of the mother tongue and of the natural sciences.

"These improvements, however, were confined entirely to the upper classes; nothing was done for the middle and lower ones.

"Next arose Henry Pestalozzi, a man of distinguished abilities, destined to point out to others the proper road by which the vices and decline of modern civilisation might be combated and subdued. His life coincided with that great event, marking the vices of European civilisation, the French revolution, in which also the democratic principle first appeared as the antagonist of the ancient aristocratic principle. Pestalozzi possessed a lively imagination, fervour of mind, a strong sense of right and of compassion for the oppressed and suffering. He first followed the profession of jurisprudence and public life; but having given offence by his hostility to the injustice of some of the political provisions of his country, and Rousseau's works on education having then appeared, he determined to follow out his views of the amelioration of the disposition and heart of man, by devoting himself to practical education. He too had his faults in this new path: he had too much dislike for learning and science; he did not sufficiently appreciate existing relations; and he did not make use enough of Christian principles, though he possessed the true Christian disposition himself. Still, we must rank him among the most distinguished men of our time, by the power and depth of his mind, by his self-sacrificing love and enthusiasm in the great cause of human improvement in spite of his disappointments, and by the impulse which he gave to education throughout Europe by his improved methods of early instruction, which still continue to work, and must do so, being founded in nature. They have also been adopted and further developed, by the successful experience of many years, by his friend Fellenberg, whose flourishing institutions are an indisputable and consoling proof of the practicability of arresting the decline of civilisation, and of preventing its anarchical tendencies. Though they are in themselves individual and local, yet having once succeeded, they are capable of being applied in any country and by any person, or even by public authority, to check the demoralising influences of a state of over-civilisation.

"Philip Emanuel von Fellenberg was born in June 1771, at Berne, of a family distinguished for patriotism and high character. His father was professor of jurisprudence, then a member of the Bernese Sovereign Council, prefect of Wildestein in the canton of Aargau, and afterwards a senator at Berne. He was as much distinguished for learning as for integrity and uprightness. His mother was the grand-daughter of the celebrated Dutch admiral Von Tromp. Her early lessons had great influence in forming the mind of Fellenberg to the love of his country and of humanity. His teachers were Rengger, afterwards minister of the interior Swiss central government, and Lereche, afterwards professor of theology at Lauzanne. He was then sent to the institution of Pfeffels at Colmar, and next to Geneva. In 1789 he went to Tübingen, where he studied jurisprudence under Hofacker, and then the philosophical sciences. On his return home he devoted himself to the classics and the Kantian philosophy. For several years he travelled over all Switzerland and the south of Germany; and having formed an early acquaintance with Pestalozzi, who was twenty-five years older than himself, he became convinced like him of the critical state of society, and its threatening demoralisation in public and private life; and that nothing could resist its ruinous tendencies but a regenerated national education among all classes. His sagacious apprehensions were fully confirmed in the outbreak of the French revolution. He went to Paris in the year 1795, which convinced him still more of the truth of his ideas. After this he devoted himself to the study of agriculture, taking no part in politics till 1798, when the revolution of Switzerland, effected by the French Directory, compelled him to join the patriots, which he did with so much zeal, that a price was set upon his head by the French commissioner Mingaud, and he was obliged to emigrate. He afterwards discharged with ability the duties of quarter-master of the upper circles of Berne. In the end of 1798 he superintended the contributions of clothes and food from the canton of Berne to that of Unterwalden, deplorably pillaged by the French. He was soon after sent by the Swiss central government to Paris, on a commission of great delicacy, where he had reason to be extremely disgusted with the conduct and principles of Reubel and Rapinat. On his return home, he purchased Hofwyl, six miles north of Berne, containing four hundred and forty Magdeburg acres,* where he entered upon his plans of agricultural and educational improvement, which he has pursued ever since, now nearly forty years, having devoted to it his whole private fortune of about 20,000*l.* His first attempts drew upon him the odium of the aristocratic party, which was suspicious of his intention, and the consequences of his plans ; and afterwards of the democratic party, which thought them equally hostile to *their* interests.

"In 1830, in consequence of the regeneration of Switzerland, he became a member of the constitution, and afterwards of the council and of the educational department, and in 1833 *landamann* of Berne, the highest office in the state, which last office he soon resigned, in order to devote himself more completely to his own institutions. These he offered to present to the state on certain considerations, in order to establish them in perpetuity ; but was prevented by the illusions, the envious and jealous passions, and the cabals of his contemporaries.

"Fellenberg cannot be understood except we go to his principles. It never was his intention merely to give to a few individuals instruction on a better plan than any other institution offered ; his intention was, to prove a principle applicable to the whole of society, that principle resting upon revealed religion as a basis, —a point too much neglected by preceding educationists. He assumed that God had created in man

* Two English acres contain three Morgen (the above-named measure) and a few square feet.

certain dispositions and faculties, by the moral training of which, together with the physical training of the body, the happiness and perfection of the individual and of society were to be brought about; according to the expression of the apostle, ' the new man, which after God is created in righteousness and true holiness.' He considered that this image might be destroyed by a perverted education, as it might be developed by an appropriate one. Labour he looked upon not in the old light of a disgrace and an evil, but as the honourable means of health and independence.

"He insisted, moreover, that the existing relations of society must be deeply respected, as founded on the will of God, till they could be improved by time,—a point which Rousseau and others had overlooked. He viewed the state as a generalisation of the family, and possessing the same principle of subordination and of mutual dependence and affection. The wisest of the ancients took the same views, as Pythagoras, Lycurgus, Plato, Aristotle, which they could not carry out fully from the absence of Christian principles. He wished the family-principle to reign in his schools, which they were to aid, and assist, and develope, but not to destroy, nor to slight and deteriorate. While he adhered thus closely to the practical routine of life, he always had in his mind's eye the great ideal perfection of the whole man and of all men, held up to us so clearly and beautifully in the Christian code, that God will have all men progress till they reach ' the measure of the fulness of the stature of Christ.'

" He allowed of no theory in education but what was inductive, according to the aphorism of Goethe, ' Believe in life; it teaches better than orator or book.'

Nor did he expect that any one system in education would solve all difficulties, or be applicable to all characters. He believed that each individual was created with a specific character and genius, which it was the duty of the educator to study and to manage; and that the peculiar disposition of each pointed out the destination intended for him by Providence. Hence he views education as a species of self-cultivation, which enables the individual to bring to perfection his peculiar talents, so that he may produce the greatest amount of good to himself and others.

"Having considered the increase of pauperism as one of the greatest evils of modern civilisation, both in itself and in its being the necessary cause of a moral and criminal degradation as extensive as itself, and indeed much more so, on account of the contagious and absorbing tendency of low moral notions,—he applied himself earnestly to the solution of the problem of physical or economical independence. He succeeded most happily in proving the practical needlessness of pauperism, by the profits of the labour of his industrial school above its expenses; and, warned by the example of Pestalozzi, that no system can prosper without a prosperous economy, he paid great attention to the profits of his own estate as one of his leading duties. He thus established the soundness and practicability of his plans by a double argument,—the education formed the moral and industrial character of the children, and the labour of the children repaid the expenses of their education. The same results might be obtained by nations now the example is before them. They might ensure the moral and religious character of their pauper-children, and their industrious independence; and the labour of these children, so trained, would repay the national outlay upon their education.

"He also shewed in his system, that it was not necessary to separate the schools for the different classes of society, but that there were great advantages in having them near each other, as it enabled the different ranks to understand their true relative position, their mutual dependence, the necessity of the distinction of ranks,—of the labourer and of the capitalist, each conferring and receiving peculiar benefits,—and the corresponding necessity for a distinct course of study and intellectual education; while a common moral feeling of kindness, charity, respect, and esteem, pervaded the whole, according to the Christian law, being all one in social harmony,—an institution never before realised, but now effectually so."

Here follows a more detailed account of the agricultural improvements of Fellenberg and of his workshops, which, having been spoken of at length in the former part of this book, need not be here repeated.

"There is this radical difference between the agricultural improvements of Fellenberg and those of the rest of Europe, and even of England. They are elsewhere considered as an END, a commercial end, of producing a better and more profitable animal or crop than can be done by the old methods. HE considers them only as *means* by which a more rational and contented disposition may be given to all classes of the community. Having increased the produce of his land sixfold, he considers it demonstrated, that we need not be alarmed at the idea of an excessive increase of population, provided their moral and industrial education be insured. Improvements cannot yet have reached their perfection, and Europe possesses much land on which no improvement has begun. Industrial occupation must be rendered honourable, in order to make the labourer respect himself and be contented, and love and respect the institutions of his country. The effect of improvements hitherto has been, in a great degree, to render the employment of the labourer more difficult and uncertain, his poverty and degradation more hopeless, and his discontent more reckless, because his spiritual nature has been almost entirely neglected.

" We must now take a view of the higher classes of society, and of their education, in the relation in which they stand to the rest. It cannot be doubted that their influence for good or evil over all the other classes is immense and almost omnipotent, from their wealth, and the moral and intellectual consequences of it. For this very reason, from the weakness of the human mind and the tendency of all power to self-abuse, their position is the more responsible and dangerous. Though commanding all other classes, they are not independent of them. Their power, indeed, consists in wielding the others as instruments; but should these instruments get into other hands, as all history shews they have done at particular periods, the very power which was a security becomes a cause of ruin; and those who direct this ruin can only calculate upon their own prospective safety by the complete annihilation, if possible, of the once-privileged class. All history teems with these lessons; but we need go no further than the French revolution for illustration, and that ought to be the more forcibly warning to us, because it threatens to be only the forerunner of a general European convulsion, from the great similarity and consanguinity of the European family of nations, unless the natural relations of the social classes are better studied and understood, and unless the minds of the higher classes themselves are made alive to the dangers of their position on the one hand, and to their highest interests and duties on the other, which are those of the friends and guardians of the other classes. This can only be done through an improved educational sentiment, of which, indeed, Christianity possesses the germ, but which, it is notorious, is altogether overlooked in all the public schools and great gymnasia of Europe. Selfishness, and pride, and a contempt for the classes below them, as they are termed, with extreme ignorance of all useful, practical knowledge, and a smattering only of the classics, are the acknowledged characteristics of the seminaries where men of rank receive the usual education; so that it has become almost proverbial, " that the children of the rich generally learn nothing." These schools do not profess to give their pupils a choice of study. They make no allowance for difference of taste, ability, or genius; nor do they inculcate humanity and charity, or benevolence, as a principle. They are limited in their masters or professors for the great purposes of education, which are the development of the character and the PECULIAR talents of individuals.

" Fellenberg combated these evils by the number of professors which he invited around him. Despising the mercantile spirit of profit upon his pupils, which is the leading principle of most other establishments, (and, in a certain sense, almost necessarily so, money being the great idol and the radical vice of European society at present, and the portentous symptom of her threatening downfal,) he returned with a liberal hand to his pupils that which they presented to him for a conventual and specific purpose. Thus, according to a pupil's rank, fortune, talents, or intended profession in life, his parents had a choice of the line of study which should engage his principal attention. For the same reasons, the classes at Hofwyl are constructed upon a different principle from that of any other institution. Sometimes a pupil studies by himself, when there is no other pursuing the same study or the same part of it, which indeed requires a greater number of teachers, and proportionably diminishes the profit of the superintendent, or the head-master, as he is called in England. But the great end of education is thus, and thus only, obtained, which is the welfare of the pupil. Schools are not instituted for the sake of the master, but for the sake of the pupils; and the perfection of the pupil's character, conduct, and intelligence, ought to be the only object aimed at, whether we consult the principles of Christianity or of common sense.

" By the number and excellence of his professors Fellenberg is able to complete the education of his higher pupils to any extent, including in it what is usually considered as the last accomplishment of a university. Some of the most celebrated literary men in Europe have been professors under him; and some of his pupils have reached the highest government-honours of their respective countries,—a proof of the soundness of the instruction.

" That his institutions have attained a general celebrity in Europe, though little known and less understood in England, is shewn in the fact, that sixteen princes have received their education there, besides the sons of men of rank and fortune in Russia, Poland, Germany, France, Italy, Spain, America, and some from England.

"In 1799 the estate of Hofwyl consisted of five houses and fifteen inhabitants. The quantity of land is now doubled; the produce multiplied sixfold; the buildings are thirteen larger and four smaller ones, capable of containing altogether six hundred persons; the population varies from 360 to 400, which is the thousandth part of the population of the canton of Berne; a number of surrounding labourers have been employed for forty years; half a million of Swiss franks have been put into circulation. The total number of pupils of the agricultural and higher scientific schools has amounted to 783; that of the poor school, the Meykirch school, and the girls' school, to 451; that of the industrial school to 210; that of the schoolmasters who receive instruction in the normal courses to 247.

"When Fellenberg commenced his establishments, he considered, from the first, that he was working for the public good, and engaged in solving one of the most important problems which could be proposed for the welfare of mankind. In 1807 he declared that he had bequeathed them in his will to the canton, as a national institution. In 1831, after the government had recognised the entire department of education in all its importance, he offered to dispose of the whole to the state upon being paid the value of the land, presenting the buildings free, which would be a calculated sacrifice to himself of about 12,000*l*., and to give the commission on whom the management might fall 500*l*. as soon as the offer was accepted. They were also to be allowed one year as a trial, during which a commission should manage the institution as a national concern. This splendid and magnanimous offer was rejected for the most frivolous reasons, probably from motives of petty jealousy and envy, the plainest facts being denied, and the results of thirty years' labour, improved land and increased population, misrepresented.

"Fellenberg wished to make Switzerland the source of the moral and educational regeneration of Europe, as her political situation and history were already remarkable. She stands in the centre of the nations; her independence is guaranteed by the other powers; she has been from early times the cradle of liberty and free institutions; she produced some of the greatest of the early reformers, Ulrich, Zwingle, and Calvin, and the great Haller, the forerunner of one large department of modern science—botany, anatomy, and medicine; she was the first to give birth to rational educational inquiries and improvements, in the persons of Rousseau and Pestalozzi, and, lastly, of Fellenberg. It is not impossible that the merits of Fellenberg may be more fully understood, and his plans adopted. Though a single individual, he may become the focus of a light which may shine over Europe and the world. It is the principle of nature to commence her grand improvements, discoveries, and inventions, in the bosoms of peculiarly distinguished individuals, and from them to benefit the whole world. Athens was but a single city, and her political power lasted a mere moment in the flow of time; but her literary riches have spread over a succession of ages, and seem destined to live as long as man himself. Judæa was once the most despised of all lands; but she gave to all a moral and religious code, which must one day touch and animate every heart on the face of the earth. So of all great discoveries, as of Guttenberg in printing, and of Jenner in the cow-pock, one individual sows the mustard-seed, which, when it has taken root, becomes the mighty and beneficent tree. If the spirit of the founder of Hofwyl should be caught by any kindred mind in any land, *there* may similar institutions arise: human nature continuing the same, born with the same faculties, subject to the same laws, developed by the same methods, the results, if law be law, cannot fail to be the same, viz. the integrity of the personal character, and its perfect harmony in all its relations, whether high or low, in whatever situation of life it may be placed; based upon Christianity and morality, reverencing established institutions, and favourable to social order, as the only condition in which it can maintain its life and vigour. If the life of that great and good man the Emperor Alexander had been spared, it was his intention to have established in Russia an institution corresponding in all its parts with that at Hofwyl, where, by assembling seminaries for all classes upon one spot, each could have been taught its own duties, and made to comprehend the mutual duties and interests of the others. Each would have seen the necessity of such a distribution of ranks and employments, and the manner in which such an arrangement contributed to the prosperity and happiness of all. Here pride and baseness, tyranny and slavery, would be alike excluded; for employment, occupation, and industry, in every degree, would be shewn to be useful and honourable. In such an institution only can the young statesman have pointed out to him the actual condition of society and its various grades: here alone can he see the *stuff* of which mankind are made; here alone can he see that every class is alike necessary and useful to the state; that all are indispensable to her security, prosperity, and greatness; and that if any one of them were wanting, or trampled upon, or set aside, a serious injury would result to the community.

"The contrast between such a place of education for a statesman, and that which is in general use, is sufficiently striking. In the latter, he is placed entirely with those of his own rank: he is accustomed to look upon himself and his class with a certain feeling of pride, and upon all the inferior classes, as they are called—those whom he is afterwards to govern, and whose happiness and welfare are to form the object of his future anxious life, with a degree of contempt; ignorant, at the same time, of their value, their character, virtues, talents, wants, and rights—for rights belong to every class of men, even in despotic countries, and much more in free ones. He then passes to a higher gymnasium or university, where he is, if possible, still more separated from practical life, and more confined to the closet; and, lastly, after many years of false views of human nature and of practical society, he has to begin the study of the facts of man, and to learn to honour and esteem those men, professions, trades, and even handicrafts, for which he has all his life felt a certain degree of contempt. Above all, he has now to learn, for the first time, (and it would be well if this were ever truly learnt, under such an isolated training,) the universal brotherhood of man; that all nations are of one stock; that every man, however mean his outward employment, has within him the mmortal spirit; that the cultivation of this spirit is the true destiny of man, to which all politics are only subservient; that the kingdoms of this world, however great and glorious in themselves, are as nothing in comparison with the glory of the spirit of man himself; that they are only the form through which this spirit is to evolve itself; that the forms are made for the spirit, not the spirit for the forms. Whoever, in the present age, cannot enter into these views of man and of his social attributes, is unfit for the crisis in which we are placed, in which the old institutions have lost their authority as a principle of action; which authority emanated from a simpler set of instincts, so to speak, and which now requires to be grounded upon rational conviction and reflection. There is reason in instinct, but the reason is not perceived while the instinct is in full vigour; but when it begins to flag, or pall upon the appetite, it requires the aid of reason to restore it to its former rights and influence.

"Happy would it be if the nations of the earth, now that the secret of the formation of character is disclosed, would prepare the way, in the language of holy writ, ' to learn war no more,' by controlling the passions and appetites in early life, by habits of early labour both practical and moral, by affording a proper food and scope for the intellectual faculties, by inculcating a rational respect and value for existing institutions, and, above all, by the universal sanction and adoption of practical Christianity, and by referring the whole character to that simple test.

"Such a consummation of modern society might seem to be Utopian and impossible, had not Fellenberg given the solution of it by an experience of forty years, and were there not strong evidences, in the midst of all our doubts and misgivings, to those who look steadily below the surface to watch the under-currents, that the constant tendencies of man in his social relations are towards a better and a higher elevation, and one which, when attained, will be less liable to revulsion and relapse.

"Happy indeed will that statesman be, and blessed will his name descend to posterity, who, looking through the mists of party to the character and nature of man himself, shall learn to respect and reverence that nature as the sublimest work of Providence; and shall consider it his own highest glory, as the instrument of that Providence, to lay the foundation of such extended institutions as may, in their effect upon national character, produce security for the highest classes, independence and content in the lowest, intelligence and integrity in all. For if life be not a dream, and the Gospel a fable, a day cannot fail of coming—we have it from unlying lips—when there shall reign 'peace on earth and good-will among men.'"

MR. CROPPER'S
AGRICULTURAL SCHOOL.

SINCE the preceding pages were put together, we have been favoured with the perusal of a small pamphlet, printed for private circulation, with the following title: "Some Account of an Agricultural School for Orphans, at Fearnhead, near Warrington, Lancashire; in a Letter to a Friend. By James Cropper. June 1839:" and as the plan can be clearly traced to the founder's acquaintance with the Swiss Institution, a notice of it may properly be included in this work.

This gentleman, a member of the Society of Friends, wished to make an experiment in order to ascertain how far labour may be rendered advantageous in training the children of the working-classes, in connexion with the usual instruction given in the National or British schools. His establishment consists of twenty-six orphans, whom he collected from the neighbouring towns: not without difficulty, because at an early age children in manufacturing towns are profitable to those to whom they belong. Hence many of those first brought to him were the idle and troublesome. After a time, some of these, by firmness and kindness, became a credit to the establishment; others continuing unmanageable and incorrigible, were returned to those from whom they were received. A certain number of children were then admitted of the ages of eight and nine, with the hope that they could be more easily trained than older boys. The first difficulty was to procure a master properly qualified to superintend both the instruction and the labour of the children; and when the younger children were taken in, additional trouble and expense were incurred, as the younger children could not labour with the older ones, and the same master could not superintend the school and the field at the same time. Another assistant was therefore necessary.

"I have always considered religion," says Mr. Cropper, "to be the basis and foundation of education and character; and next to this, habits of order and steady industry, though these are rather the development and proofs of religious principle, than a separate unconnected department. I wished at first to attain my object of forming the character, from motives of gratitude and duty alone; but I have found by experience, that such ignorant, neglected, and untutored minds, as have come under our care, require other more cogent and self-interested motives to induce them to self-exertion. I therefore appropriated to them nine acres of land rent-free: the whole labour of which is performed by themselves, under the superintendence of the master, who keeps an account of the labour performed by each boy, and rates and pays for it per rod, as if done by hired labourers. Two-thirds of what is thus earned is passed to the credit of the school, and the remainder is divided among the boys in proportion to the share of labour performed by each. The profits, if any arise from the produce, are shared by the master and boys: one-third being allotted to the former in addition to his salary, and two-thirds to the latter. This sum is invested for the use of the boys at a future day. At the end of 1838, the profit from the nine acres was 60*l*., which was apportioned as above. I have since allotted to them about fifty acres more land, which is at present in a low state of cultivation, and for which I shall charge a moderate rent. The same arrangement is followed with these as with the nine acres; and it is probable the whole profit may be double that of last year, which will make a profit to each boy of nearly 3*l*. Up to the present time (six months), the earnings have been at the rate of about 6*l*. per annum, of which 2*l*. will be placed to their credit, and 4*l*. to that of the establishment.

"The cost of food, clothing, and education, is 12*l*. per annum each; but if the above estimate is realised, it will be reduced to 8*l*. each; and if the whole profit of their labour was placed to the credit of the school, it would reduce the cost to 3*l*. each. My object, however, was to serve the children; and I thought the best way of doing it was to give them an interest in the prosperity of the concern.

"Should the boys be disposed to pursue the employment of agriculture, my ultimate object is to settle them in small farms of three acres each. If they remain with me till they are eighteen or nineteen, or older, it would both increase their pecuniary advantages, and benefit the establishment. If any of them, when old enough to judge for themselves, should prefer some other occupation, I shall endeavour, if their conduct has been satisfactory, to place them suitably. It is fully understood by them, that no boy, who leaves the establishment without my approbation, will have any advantage from the money placed to his credit.

"I will now consider that very serious and important question, which lies at the root of the moral and physical improvement of the working-classes,—viz. how far manual labour promotes or hinders school learning and mental cultivation with children of the working-classes. After the experience of several years, I have no hesitation in deciding that the labour, which occupies two-thirds of the children's time, does not prevent their acquiring a sufficient knowledge of reading, spelling, writing, arithmetic, together with the rudiments of grammar, geography, geometry, and natural history. Their acquaintance with Scripture is also considerable; and I believe their acquirements in general are at least equal to those of the children of the national or British schools.

" We find that constant steady employment has a very favourable influence upon the general conduct of the boys. Their favourite pursuit is field-labour; but when, from the state of the weather, or other causes, they are more confined to school, they apply to their studies with much greater interest and cheerfulness than if they had had no intermission. We have indeed reason to be gratified with their improvement in every respect."

PRACTICAL DETAILS.

"The produce and prices of the following statement may possibly appear to some to be excessive; but it must be recollected, that we are in those respects favourably situated. We have a ready sale for early vegetables: Bolton and Manchester afford an extensive market; and farther to the east there is a dense population, where the land is unproductive, and the crops late.

" In 1837, being the first year of the establishment, potatoes averaged 362 bushels of 84 lbs. per acre. In 1838, owing to the unfavourable season, we got only 240 bushels per acre.

"In 1837, the average crops of turnips and mangel wurzel were as under:

Sown turnips	40 tons per acre.
Once transplanted	26 ,,
Twice transplanted	16 ,,
Best sown mangel	28 ,,
Late ditto	13 ,,

"The above is the weight of the roots of mangel wurzel, some of the leaves having been gathered whilst growing. In 1838, the turnips produced were, some 40 tons per acre, some 26; a larger proportion 20; some less. The season was very unfavourable for mangel wurzel; none of the land produced more than 14 tons of roots, and 19 tons of leaves per acre.

"The average of vetches produced on an acre, during these two years, would keep one cow 190 days; and they were cut in time to be followed by transplanted Swedish turnips.

"Early potatoes, in the same time, produced from 20*l.* to 30*l.* per acre; autumn-sown onions much more; cabbages and peas full as much as the potatoes;—all of which were got off in time for a good crop of transplanted Swedish turnips.

"Strawberries and raspberries have been very productive. Good crops of strawberries have realised at the rate of 80*l.* per acre; raspberries and black currants have produced fully 50*l.* per acre; apples and pears, where the trees are in full bearing, are also likely to be a source of considerable profit, as well as other kinds of fruit in common use;—I should suppose about 40*l.* per acre."

All the English and French publications, together with some German ones, on Hofwyl, have been consulted by the Author, who has also had the advantage of reading several of the letters of De Fellenberg, though not addressed to himself. The representations contained in those various works have been corrected by the observations of more recent eye-witnesses. Amongst the most valuable of the authorities should be named that of the Rev. W. C. Woodbridge, whose articles on Hofwyl, in the American "Annals of Education," deserve to be republished in England.

If this little work be favourably received, the Author intends to prepare for publication some details of Ridolfi's Agricultural Institution, near Florence; of the "Colonie Agricole" at Mettray, near Tours, in France; and of some rural labour-schools in England.

www.ingramcontent.com/pod-product-compliance
Lightning Source LLC
LaVergne TN
LVHW061216060426
835507LV00016B/1954